GI Odyssey

GI Odyssey

World War II Memoir/Novella

Harold Flagg

ex-U.S. Army T/Sgt.
771st Constabulary Squadron
and
771st Tank Battalion
"Tanks" for the Memories

France Switzerland Germany England

Washington, D.C. New York Boston Ozark Mountains Miami
French Canada "Margaritaville" Key West
and Toledo, OH

To order additional copies of this book, contact:
Xlibris Corporation
1-888-795-4274
www.Xlibris.com
Orders@Xlibris.com
38036

CONTENTS

To all of our military—past, present, and future: Thanks.

PREFACE

Why do we kill
when we could just chill?
Trash the slaughter!
It's so much cheaper
to pleasure one another.

And yet I must admit.
War was the perfect fit
for my coming-of-age
in a cage of rage.

Harold Flagg

1

Slow Boat to Hell

You can hurtle yourself backwards or forwards in time in your mind's eye—what is known as "mental time travel."
—Jessica Marshall, Cover Story,
NewScientist (March 24-30, 2007)

High school senior Harry "Harold Flagg" Bandera was the ultimate geek and a frequent target of bullies. They pleasured themselves by calling him Daddy Long Legs and making sport of his skinny-Minnie body. His breath, as little kids say today, "would knock over a freakin' bull."

Despite all of the above, Harry's top priority was to drop out of high school and join the college-oriented Army Specialized Training Program. He saw the ASTP as his only shot at being the first in his family to go to college.

As it turned out, he had an ASTP brain, but not the body. So he was deemed unfit for military duty and sent back to the family farm. He felt forever saddled with such soul-searing dead-end jobs as hoeing corn, slopping hogs, cleaning chicken coops, gathering eggs, and the weekly decapitation of chickens to be plucked, dressed, and fried for Sunday dinner.

His summer of discontent ended after his draft number came up in October 1944. He once again had to face a round of medical tests and psychological probes along lines of "Do you like girls?" So one more time, he traveled by rail from hometown Toledo to a District 5 recruiting center in Cleveland. During the trip, he literally "went bananas" in the hope that this would add enough weight to tip the scales in his favor.

He never should have bothered.

The draft board, it turned out, was having difficulties fulfilling its quota. If that meant lowering standards, then so be it. He probably failed his medical exam, but got drafted anyway; said good-bye to family and friends at Toledo Union Station; and entrained for Camp Atterbury, Indiana.

After formal induction as a U.S. Army buck private, he was issued GI—government issue—uniforms, boots, underwear, socks, the works! After many tests and psychological evaluations, he was assigned to Signal Corps training at Camp Crowder, near Joplin, Missouri.

Almost from the get-go, Harry caught on to such military axioms as "hurry up and wait" and "never volunteer." He became expert at avoiding drill sergeants who had a way of coming out of nowhere, extending a forefinger, and demanding as a prelude to disaster: "I want three volunteers—you, you, and you."

Harry became proficient at "hospital corners." Knowing how to tuck in bedsheets with military precision is something that remains with you forever—not unlike your first view of Paris from the top of the Eiffel Tower. An improperly made bed, or a belt threaded from the right instead of the left, meant a "gig," followed by KP—or kitchen patrol—instead of a weekend pass to paint the town red, white, and blue.

Day after day, Harry felt and looked more fit, thanks to plenty of push-ups, sit-ups, and calisthenics, also known as calijumptics. He felt more and more able to load full combat gear on his "GI aching back" and then march up and down Ozark hillsides. On the other hand, he wasn't too tickled about scrambling up, over, and down obstacle-course barricades. Nor was he gung ho about crawling like a baby under barbed wire, while live ammunition was fired just a few inches above his head and butt.

Frequent hikes and gymnastic gyrations galore called for nutritious high-protein food—lots and lots of all he could eat. Within weeks after his physical makeover, he morphed into a handsome tall trim young man who looked in a mirror and said, "If I get killed in the war, I will make a good-looking corpse." That's exactly the thought of ancient Greek poet Tyrtæus, who wrote,

> The youth's fair form is fairest when he dies.
> Even in his death, the boy is beautiful,
> The hero boy who dies in his life's bloom.
> He lives in men's regret and women's tears.
> More sacred than in life, more beautiful by far,
> Because he perished on the battlefield.

During boot camp, Harry thought about dying—a lot. How would he pass away? Would a German U-boat fire a torpedo at his troopship and kill everybody on board? His mind tuned in on eardrum-piercing bombards bursting in air, followed by severed limbs and torn-apart heads flying through the gunpowder-scented air. He could smell burning flesh and hear the screams of men not quite dead yet.

Then he remembered how a drowning person runs out of oxygen and dies. Such a death seemed relatively painless, more or less like being what fellow farmers called drunk as a skunk. Yes, he reasoned, that would be the best of all possible send-offs.

But what about dying on dry land? He pictured himself with GI comrades when a grenade, about to explode, landed near his feet. There was only one thing to do—become a hero, albeit a dead hero, and throw his body over the grenade before it blew up. Shortly thereafter, he would be the lone soldier to be blown to bits, and the others would be saved.

By the end of April 1945, it was time to "shape up and ship out," as drill sergeants liked to order. On Harry's last stateside evening, he posed for a portrait in Boston, then left Richards Studio and went looking for the bus stop at Pack Square. No wonder he was having trouble! The Bostonian words "Pack Square" turned out to be *Park* Square.

While waiting for the bus back to camp, Harry indulged in a shoeshine. At one point, he was asked where he was headed. When an answer was refused, the shoeshine man realized his mistake and apologized for asking the wrong question, namely, top secret information.

It seemed like everything nowadays was top secret. Everybody knew that a troopship was in the harbor, but nobody had a clue as to where it was headed. So it was back to camp and a ride next morning to a POE—port of embarkation—at Atlantic Pier, Boston. It was there that Harry and comrades were packed like cords of wood in former luxury liner SS *Mariposa*, currently refitted as a troop transport.

Once aboard, the vibes were strong and scary. Harry knew only that he was on a ship headed for God knew where. And for some, it would be a one-way trip. The situation was made all the more ominous because of posters showing Uncle Sam with his finger pressed against his lips as he whispered, "A slip of the lip can sink a ship."

Harry began to daydream about peacetime life back on the farm. How simple and tranquil life once seemed! He now had orders to shoot, maim, and kill his opponents, and not just yell football-game threats such as "Burnham high, Burnham low, burn their a—and watch 'em go."

Burnham High School was a two-story brick institution where Harry's favorite school subjects were journalism, Latin, and Spanish—the better to prepare for his dream job as a foreign correspondent. He reveled in Pan-American Union literature and President Franklin Delano Roosevelt's Good

Neighbor policy. Harry liked to picture himself as cast in the Walt Disney film *Saludos Amigos*, as he watched cowboys galloping across the Wild West Argentine Pampa, out-of-control rumba dancers "in the groove and looking good," milewide waterfalls, tropical trees rife with orchids, rain forests chockablock with monkeys swinging a la Tarzan from tree to tree, jet-black panthers languishing under a starlit night in a tropical rain forest, lost cities in desolate deserts, or the towering snowcapped Andes.

Latin American studies replaced Harry's Slavic heritage that was lost due to a divorce, charging desertion. The divorce meant that his mother, Florence May "Florrie" Wheatley Slusarczyk-Salin, was banished from the Anglican Catholic—or American High Episcopal-Church. Florrie was not allowed to celebrate Holy Communion or any other holy sacrament, especially marriage. That didn't stop her from falling in love and eventually marrying Ohio farmer Wesley "Wayne" Flagg. Not long thereafter, Gladys Flagg was born as a half sister to the Salin siblings—Robert George and Harold "Harry Bandera" Salin. The Salins eventually would adopt the family name Flagg.

Meanwhile, back on the ship, Harry programmed his mind to recall the first home he could remember. It was a two-story, four-room frame house with neighboring chicken coops, a highly productive English walnut tree, storage cribs filled with corn and rats, a silo, and a thirty-foot-high barn for livestock and alfalfa hay. The hay—plus grain—was fed daily to pigs, cows, chickens, and two horses. Others "at table" included pet rabbits and the occasional opossum—nasty tempered though these and other feral creatures can be.

A twenty-dollar monthly crop-share income went for "store-bought" food, clothes, and basic necessities. During winter months, the money bought fuel oil to heat a living room and one of two upstairs bedrooms. The family's most prized furnishings featured an antique hutch of Early American design and a rosewood piano from England. The piano was spinet sized in the European style; American pianos were twice as large. Bronze candlesticks graced the piano's music rack. It was gorgeous, but useless. During its sea voyage from England, salt water corroded the piano's strings. Unfortunately, there was no money for repairs. Eventually the piano was sold to an antique dealer.

Weekly delivery of a fifty-cent chunk of ice kept food fresh for several days. An occasional Friday fish fry, courtesy of fresh-caught fish sold from the trunk of a Lake Erie fisherman, became a major treat. A dark, dank, chilly cellar was chockablock with homemade pickles, canned fruit, and tomatoes in recently invented Mason jars, crocks of cheese, pails of milk, homemade wine, and something called head cheese—a culinary hodgepodge that Harry hated. It comprised such porcine parts as ears, snout, fat, and skin. As pig farmers put it, "Nothing goes to waste except the squeal."

The annual hog butchering was a community project. First, the pig's skull was crushed by a blow from Granddad Charley Flagg's sledgehammer. Then the animal's throat was slit, entrails removed, and the carcass dumped into a big iron pot of boiling water.

Summertime "thrashing" of wheat was the most festive of farm events. Harry clearly remembered the community-owned thresher machine that separated wheat from straw. The processed grain and straw was then stored away for future use. Hard work under a red-hot sun put sweaty threshers in the mood for stick-to-the-ribs cookery washed down by iced tea. Churchgoing farm women forbid the serving of strong drink, but sometimes a beer or three would slip through security, such as it was. Most of the younger workers doffed their shirts, but his "un-Christian" seminudity and lack of modesty was accepted or oftentimes ignored.

Each housewife worked hard for laurels as host with the most. A certain housewife might be famous for luscious lemon chiffon pie or maybe premium pineapple upside-down cake, another for crispy peppery fried chicken, or someone else for cinnamon-spiced apple pie, complete with a slice of homemade cheese. After-dinner coffee had to be "strong enough to put hair on your chest."

A Delco generator was the biggest single expenditure for Harry's family. The contraption provided power for electric lights and a wonderful radio with a tiny yellow dial light—the last word in high tech of that time. Evenings often meant a time to sit on the floor and listen to the radio spinning adventures like those of the Lone Ranger and Tonto. Harry developed a taste for scary stories that kicked off with "who knows what evil lurks in the hearts of men? The Shadow knows."

His number 1 weekend must was a program beginning with the song: "Here's to *Your Hit Parade* and the tunes that you picked to be played."

Stepfather Wayne would complain about the "modern" songs. "You call that noise music? In my day, they had real words you could understand, like 'every little breeze seems to whisper Louise.'" The latter tune was Wayne's favorite—if somewhat dated—pop song.

Harry suspected that his people were poor, but didn't know for certain until he saw his first motion picture. It featured a song and dance act starring a little girl called Shirley Temple, complete with banana curls. In the background were leather lounge chairs and other elegant furnishings much fancier than anything he had ever seen before.

During Great Depression years, a free movie became a major social event that took place every Monday at dusk, weather permitting. Country-store merchants—what few there were—hoisted a bedsheet in a vacant lot. A projector subsequently flashed motion pictures, complete with sound. There were no chairs. The mostly young audience sat, or sprawled out, on the grass.

Being poor didn't stop Florrie's house from being a home, with all the warmth and coziness that word evokes. Five days a week, she packed school lunches for three. She cooked daily meals on a big black coal- and wood-burning stove. Somehow, she managed her household with only a minibudget based on the family's share of farm crops, eggs, and livestock. (Later in life, Harry became aware that money management is a British genetic skill, as witness Anglo-style financial centers including London, Bermuda, Cayman Islands, Singapore, Hong Kong, The Bahamas, Turks and Caicos Islands, and Alexandria during the reign of British-backed King Farouk.)

On at least one occasion, the Methodist minister came to Florrie's for Sunday dinner. Sunday was feast day, a time when Ohio Buckeyes of the former New France ate as well as the French do on a daily basis. Harry's mom spent quite a few hours preparing mouthwatering roast chicken, gizzard gravy, buttery mashed potatoes, garden-fresh vegetables, and a tasty cake or pie dessert. After all, a man of God as Sunday dinner guest was an honor reserved for the church's most respected cooks.

Aside from dress-up Sunday dinner with the preacher, Harry's family also cleaned up well for programs at Farley Methodist Episcopal Church, located several miles away from home. Car pooling made church and Sunday school events accessible.

The family's only alternate travel options were a horse and buggy—and a cantankerous Willys-Overland. The latter was sabotaged before a proposed belling, or *charivari*, New France Ohio word for an after-wedding beer party. Florrie didn't need a beer bust. Nor did she care to meet the local drinkers of strong beverages. So she and her new husband chose to escape by car as soon as they heard "bellers" ringing bells to announce upcoming boozing and socializing. The newlyweds ran toward the family's best transportation—the aforementioned Willys. However, the Willys had been sabotaged, something about a missing generator. So they hitched Colonel—the horse—to a buggy. Harry was visiting Grandma Wheatley, so he missed the escape escapade; his brother Bob got more than he had expected however. Bob was seated in the back of the buggy, just under the buckboard. As Colonel galloped across fields and crossed an irrigation ditch, Bob's head bounced up and hit the buggy's buckboard. As a result, he was unconscious for the remainder of the flight to Grandma Wheatley's house. The only other casualty was a rural free delivery mailbox. It got in the buggy's way and was subsequently trashed. An apology and replacement ended the affair to everyone's satisfaction—except for the thwarted planners of one heck of a beer bash.

Far more fun than a beer party was the Christmas celebration at Farley ME Church. Every Christmas, each kid received an orange wrapped in brightly colored tissue paper. It evoked sunny Florida with its palm-fringed tropical beaches.

The two brothers shared a second-floor bedroom. Harry spent countless hours staring at the south window and daydreaming about palm-fringed beaches in storybook places like Tahiti. Family friend May Kopitke gave Harry a copy of *Mutiny on the Bounty*, and it filled his mind with thoughts of a tropical Eden where summer spent the winter. Blizzards, windows draped in icicles, and roads coated in frozen snow, plus traveling to see a Toledo Museum of Art painting by Paul Gauguin, reinforced his longing for tropical sunshine and pink-sand stretches of lonely beaches. His favorite toy was a boat that he sailed to imaginary cities and islands in the farm's irrigation ditch. To him, a muddy make-believe harbor and a stone Sugarloaf Mountain represented a virtual Rio de Janeiro. After a short stay in Rio, he pretended to tour Hawaii before going to Africa and going on safari just like Hemingway and his pals. Then he might split for Florida, where Ohio's rich people, plus robins and orioles, exchanged winter for summer.

A warm fragrant spring shower in the nearby woods created tiny lakes fringed in mayapples—a wildflower with leaves that resembled palm fronds. Harry thought of the minilakes as Tahitian lagoons where beautiful brown men and women went skinny-dipping in crystal clear tropical waters.

April showers brought Virginia-spring-beauty flowers. They formed a pink and white floral carpet at the woods entrance. Then there was soul-restoring hawthorn bush, always at its fragrance zenith during the first days of spring. Aside from the return of robins, springtime was initially announced by pussy willows sprouting and blooming on the sides of irrigation ditches. Harry thought Ohio's wildflowers of springtime had to be the world's prettiest. But Florrie favored her native England's Crayola-colored primroses.

In the late spring and early summer, there was a wild display of mostly green jack-in-the-pulpits, highly perfumed lilies of the valley, pink and white trillium, and violets in shades of—well—violet.

On the last day of primary school, it was traditional for the teacher to host a woodland picnic complete with roasted marshmallows and hot dogs.

Everything about the setting was picture-postcard-perfect, especially the rustic log fence that zigzagged around the forest entrance. The woods faced an unpaved thoroughfare disrespectfully known as Mud Road. Harry liked to wander along the road and be all to himself except for bobolinks sounding the musical greeting: *bobolink, spink, spank, spink.*

Right after a warm spring shower, the family went looking for its special treat—sponge mushrooms that ringed the bottom of tree trunks in the apple orchard. Aside from butter-fried morels, the best garden treat was the sun-warmed tomato for which Ohio was famous.

What Ohio didn't have was pineapples. As a matter of culinary history, this tropical fruit was like caviar, served only to the wealthy; hence a pineapple became the symbol of first-class hospitality. Pineapple pie was the best dessert he had ever tasted. Once, during KP at officers' mess, Harry downed two pineapple pies and got terribly ill. He knew it was no use reporting to sick bay. That would have meant confessing to the theft of pies meant for commissioned officers—not a mere buck private.

There was nothing as effective as certain scents to make Harry's mind go into high gear. After savoring the fragrance of fresh-baked pineapple pie, his nose switched to salt-scented air that he alone enjoyed during his nighttime gig on U-boat patrol. All was well, as if the world was at peace, not war. And oh, the privacy! That was the best part. It made him think of an army ditty that goes

> Why do they call a private a "private"?
> When there's nothing less private on earth.
> The whole United Nations can hear your conversations,
> And read your mail and borrow your underwear.
> Who's got my *Collier's*?

The latter referred to a popular magazine featuring star reporter Ernest Hemingway—one of the most celebrated warrior-writers since Homer in ancient Greece.

Rather than think some more about death and destruction, Harry tuned in childhood joys such as walks in the woods with a lively beagle named Popeye. The cunning canine had been put up for adoption because a cat had scratched out her eye. Although pedigreed and pricey, Popeye was too unattractive to score a wealthy owner.

Popeye, nevertheless, was more than an expert rabbit hunter, for which beagles are especially bred. She was a first-class bird dog as well. Harry spent wonderful times watching Popeye scare up feral rabbits, squirrels, and splendiferous "cockbirds." The latter were as proud as they were beautiful. After pheasants were brought down with a scattering of buckshot, their throats were slit, and the bird was bled dry. Harry was intrigued by the proud and brave way the bird would hold high his head, right up to the moment of death. He hoped he would die as courageously if and when he was killed in the war.

Harry began to contemplate the irony behind his journey from America to Europe, just as his mother—also a teenager—had left her English homeland. She set sail on the British luxury liner SS *Mauretania*, aka Queen of the Seas. And now family history was repeating, only in reverse!

Speaking of Florrie, her liberal values used to stir up a major controversy after she welcomed Jews into her farmhouse! This was a no-no. To make matters worse, Florrie had no compunctions about breaking bread—that is, sitting at table—with Jews.

One of Florrie's special Jewish friends—let us call her Ruth—was a regular customer for eggs, free-range chickens, and talk of the Great War. Ruth felt comfortable with Florrie, since both women knew about wartime cruelty and insanity. After all, Florrie's Gorcott Hall home had been bombed by a German zeppelin. The bomb turned out to be a dud, or Harry wouldn't be here.

"Ruth could talk to me," Florrie said, "but not to others who never knew about awful things that happen during wartime. She even told me about the night Bolsheviks broke into her home, grabbed her naked baby boy by his legs, took out a sword, and stopped the boy's screams by slicing it in half, right before her eyes. Then she was beat up, tossed in a pit, and sprinkled with lime. She still has nightmares and can't talk to most people about it, only to people like me who know about war.

"After she was left for dead, someone noticed Ruth was still alive, and she was rescued. Then Ruth's dream was to somehow escape Russia and go to America. The U.S. immigration quota for Russians was filled up, but the Canadian quota would still let her come to Canada and then wait to find a way to move on to America. And now, she is one of my best chicken-and-egg customers. I don't know what we would do without my chicken money coming in every week."

Perhaps, Harry figured, Florrie survived and thrived during the latest world war because she knew how to benefit from her World War I experiences. Instead of a WWII Victory Garden, she had grown fresh produce at the family's eight-hundred-year-old ancestral home, Gorcott Hall. On "state occasions," as she put it, Florrie wore her Women's Land Army decoration from His Imperial Majesty George V, King of the United Kingdom of Great Britain and Ireland and Emperor of India.

After World War I came to an end, most Wheatley and Yeomans adult males had been killed or had fled to lands with a more promising future. One of Harry's great-uncles went to Transvaal in South Africa to seek his fortune in gold. Shortly after arrival in Africa, he suffered a fatal heart attack. Another ancestor went to New Zealand. According to family lore, this transplanted "kiwi" died and had the best-attended funeral locals could recall. Yet another great-uncle—Victorian families tended to be large—became a *Times of Ceylon* editor in Colombo, capital of British Ceylon.

Immediately after the Great War of 1914-1918, everything went to hell. Gone with the wind was the wealth and comfort of Edwardian England. There followed a Spanish flu epidemic that killed people by the millions.

The U.S. quota for English immigrants was wide open, so the Wheatleys had relatively few visa problems as they packed up and left for America. They took with them what little money remained in their name and a rosewood piano with brass candlesticks. The latter was the finest piece of furniture in the Wheatley-Yeomans ancestral home, Gorcott Hall. This Tudor-style farm mansion dated to the twelfth century and was said to have been a rest stop for Queen Elizabeth I during a trip to visit her boyfriend in Kenilworth Castle. Good Queen Bess is credited with leaving behind her coat of arms painted on glass and installed in the window of Gorcott's largest room. Gorcott Hall was also a battlefield in the civil war that followed the beheading of England's King. Over the years, several cannonballs have been found on Gorcott property. They were leftover from a battle in which the ditches ran red with blood, hence the name of the nearby town of Redditch—all one word. Sometimes Florrie pronounced it "red itch."

Aside from a sense of humor and free-spirited maverick attitude, Florrie possessed another perfect solution for a bad situation. On such occasions, she would "draw some water, put the kettle on the stove, and brew a fresh cup of tea." Nine times out of ten, the latest crisis would disappear just after the last sip of hot tea.

Harry thought it must have taken gallons and gallons of tea to get his mother through the stress of exchanging the comforts of Edwardian England for a pioneer's life in the New World. First off, the Wheatleys had been convinced that America's streets were paved in gold. Upon arrival in the United States, they found some streets were actually mud roads. Florrie and her sister went back to their hotel room and spent their first day producing torrents of hot tears. After a good cry, Gladys vowed a return to England and "marry a millionaire."

Florrie set out to find information on the wonderful town of Toledo. That was where the British Wheatley and Yeomans families had a wealthy distant relative they called Uncle George. He was to provide them with a farm home near Toledo. To make a long story short, the Wheatleys became forever grateful for Uncle George's role in providing a home base for a search to find a better life in America. However, when Harry first met Uncle George, he was dismayed by the man's favorite dish—English-style sparrow pie. Many birds had to be killed to provide this delicacy imported from English farms. Another point: Uncle George trashed Sunday school teachings by having more than an occasional glass of port—the fortified wine from England's dearest, oldest ally Portugal. Uncle George also honored the English tradition of naming not only people but cars, farms, and homes. He called his eighty-acre Ohio spread Evendale Farm. Its location was just west of the state's third largest city—the Great Lake port named Toledo after the famed swords of Toledo, Spain.

Only thing was, Florrie didn't know how to pronounce "Toledo." She called it "tolly dough." No one in New York had ever heard of Tolly Dough. So it was back to the hotel and more tears and more "English" tea. And it must be hot tea. Florrie thought the American penchant for iced drinks caused stomach ailments, maybe even ulcers. Florrie's pet name for iced tea became American champagne.

Future Grandma Wheatley was the family's least Americanized and most "set in her ways." She was upset by the American penchant for corn on the cob. "Only pigs and Americans eat maize," she would snort. Maize is the English word for corn, and it was considered food fit only for nonhuman animals.

Florrie was amused by Americans who insisted that they spoke English. At best, she found that the Yanks speak something that could only be called American English, chockablock with grunts like "uh-huh" instead of a yes.

Sloppy English notwithstanding, the American Roaring Twenties economy started to live up to its reputation as the Era of Wonderful Nonsense. Jane Elizabeth "Jenny" Wheatley and daughters took to the 1920s like sharks in a feeding frenzy. Uncle George's Tin Lizzie—a black horseless carriage or "flivver"—became the centerpiece for the Wheatley family's restored peace and plenty. Older people spoke of an automobile as "the machine."

At Christmastime, a year-old plum pudding was taken from the cellar—half-drowned in rum and brandy "hard sauce"—and served as the same dessert that had graced Yuletide British tables during the British Empire's Golden Age. Equally traditional as Christmas plum pudding was the lighting of a fresh-cut pine tree. Tiny pastel-colored candles were set in tin holders. Then the candles were lighted with "safety" matches. The family enjoyed the

Yuletide glow for a few minutes on Christmas Eve and then the candlelights were put out and the decorations packed away and out of sight. Also put in storage was a fresh-baked plum pudding, which would become next year's holiday pud. Actually, it was more of a fruitcake than a pudding. English food names often confuse their American cousins. For example, Yorkshire pudding isn't really a pudding. Chips are called french fries in America; our potato chips are "crisps." "Come by and knock me up" means a wake-up call, English style.

Aunt Gladys knew all the latest slang words and was the family glamour girl. She was first to bob her hair. She heated curling irons to just the right temperature to give her "do" some Roaring Twenties "bling." At Christmastime, she didn't mind what Santa Claus brought her, as long as it was Evening in Paris perfume—widely advertised as "the scent of luxury." Aunt Gladys scored the best Christmas gifts because of her birthday—December 27. That called for expensive gifts coming from Father Christmas as a Happy Birthday as well as a Happy Christmas—or even Happy Boxing Day, the traditional English celebration every December 26.

Gladys was good—real good—at tennis, her favorite sport and one usually associated with the rich and successful. She helped her son William Victor take tennis to its highest level. The second son, Howard, inherited the scientific smarts of his entomologist German American father, Ferdinand "Ferd" F. Dicke. Uncle Ferd was to become Harry's favorite relative. The apple of Uncle Ferd's eye was only daughter Catherine Jane. She subsequently became known as Susie.

The Wheatley sisters went all out for fashions and passions of the twenties. Florrie, egged on by her younger sister, Gladys, bobbed her dark brown hair, hiked her skirt, applied a touch or three of rouge and lipstick—a privilege once reserved for "painted ladies." Both siblings got a kick—pun intended—out of Charleston tunes with silly but catchy lyrics like "You're my hotsy, I'm your totsy, ev'rything is hotsy totsy now."

Harry's first childhood musical recollections comprised the one and two, one and two, beat of the Charleston song and dance. Even as a youngster, he could shake his booty with all the panache of Polish American Charleston star Gilda Gray—It Girl and Shimmy Queen of the Roaring Twenties.

Then came the stock market meltdown of 1929, and the economy tanked. Almost everybody seemed to be financially embarrassed, without credit, and often as not, suicidal and drowning in debt. Harry's family survived—even thrived—by growing their own food, making their own clothes, beer, wine, paraffin wax for canning, and other homemade products. Listening to the radio, playing board games, and just plain conversation provided an ample source of free entertainment. Harry's family was "on relief," as welfare was called in the days long before food stamps. That meant Florrie had access to such treasures as big bags of flour and sometimes small bags of sugar. Actually, the Depression wasn't all that depressing. Harry reveled in such ten-cent treasures as Big Little Books about Flash Gordon, Buck Rogers, and Dick Tracy—these publications being forerunners of the comic books to come.

Many years later, when he was in his early twenties, Florrie and Harry reminisced about Depression times; and Florrie said, slowly and softly, "I think we had more fun back then."

By 1939, the world was back in the war business. Suddenly there were jobs and money, but nothing to rival the income tax-free days of the 1920s.

Harry was fourteen and watching a Sylvan Theater movie on Sylvania's Main Street when Japan attacked the United States at Pearl Harbor, Hawaii. When Harry and his brother left the theater, they could sense something was wrong. There was an eerie silence in the streets and only one topic—"We are at war, may God help us." At that time, Harry and his brother never imagined that they would be among troops in two wars—Harry in World War II and Bob in the Korean Conflict. Bob, incidentally, entered the navy under his father's surname and the army under his stepfather's last name.

Harry conceded that his mom had done more to win the war than anyone else in the family. Florrie processed countless tin cans to be recycled as war material. She put up crock after crock of lard destined to become explosives. Even aluminum toothpaste tubes were recycled. She was especially adept at using ration coupons. Gasoline was rationed, but the government gave all farmers A stickers that more than covered the family's fuel needs. Gasoline availability was so important that cars and trucks were issued window tags reading "Is This Trip Really Necessary?"

Florrie had more than enough sugar ration coupons. That was because the family maintained about thirty colonies of three-banded Italian bees—one of the most productive of honeybee varieties.

No one in the family went hungry because they killed and butchered hogs for the cellar larder, shot and dressed venison, canned tomatoes, pickled cucumbers, churned butter, turned fats and lye into homemade soap bars, shucked walnuts, and even sterilized pig intestines before stuffing them with sausage meat. Washing and sterilizing Mason jars was almost a sacred ritual vital to food preservation during Ohio's long freezing-cold winters. Recycling was practiced long before it became twenty-first century popular. Florrie saved aluminum wrap and egg cartons for frequent reuse.

Although the Methodist Church WCTU—Women's Christian Temperance Union—frowned on strong drinks, many farm women grew hops to flavor barrels of home brew. They also made elderberry and cherry wines by the gallons.

The family's tiny income sufficed even for school books and supplies, as well as the latest style in hats for Harry and Bob. Both boys were delighted with their hats just like those worn by Killer Dillinger and Pretty Boy Floyd—among the most publicized of bank robbers fighting Depression poverty in all the wrong ways.

War-fueled prosperity eventually made it possible to move from substandard housing to a new home. It had hot and cold running water, a coal-burning furnace that provided central heating, washing machine, cistern, a freezer, and even a machine that plucked feathers from chickens to be sold to city folk. Such modern conveniences made time for Florrie's almost daily letters to wherever Harry happened to be stationed.

Mail call was the best of GI happy hours. The older men liked to show off perfumed envelopes containing love letters from young women they had left behind. Sometimes a "Dear John" letter would break off an engagement. This usually inspired world-class cursing episodes.

Harry learned to type at Burnham High, where he was the only boy in a class of twenty-five young women. At that time, young women were expected to get office jobs rather than become workaholic farm wives. So what does the army do? They send Harry, already an excellent typist, to a Signal Corps typing class. After typing to music, it was time for climbing telephone poles. Harry skinned his knees and damaged his fatigues more than once while learning to climb telephone poles. He much preferred brainier Signal Corps studies—like Morse code, cryptography, spying, and the protection of classified documents. He took great pride in the orange braid newly sewn on his PX-bought service cap. Like most GIs, he hated official headgear, known in the vernacular as c—t caps. That was because the caps evoked a part of female anatomy not mentioned in polite society. It was a common practice to go to the post exchange—or PX—and buy a more stylish headgear. Harry's cap subsequently was trimmed in orange braid rather than the blue on infantrymen's caps. The infantry, incidentally, was honored as Queen of the Battlefield, and the field artillery was King—the unit "that put the balls where the Queen wants them." Unfortunately, a few wrong clicks on an artillery piece and soldiers died, courtesy of the most idiotic of military oxymora—friendly fire.

Army orientation courses were optional, but Harry attended every one for which he could find the time. The courses often featured films highlighting social disease sores, scabs, and scars. Sometimes there was just a hint of what went on in Nazi camps where Jews—and others—were tortured, starved, and/or put to death. Little by little, there were more and more horror stories about Nazi atrocities. For the most part, these tales were too horrible to accept as truth rather than propaganda.

Harry's AGCT—or Army General Classification Test—score was supposed to be confidential information. But he snooped around and found out his score was the second highest in his entire battalion. That's a lot of men. As he learned in orientation sessions, platoons were organized as companies, companies as battalions, and battalions of around six hundred men became divisions. Next in line was a regiment. A bunch of regiments formed an army, like General George "Blood and Guts" Patton's Third Army. Ah, yes, Patton—he who was famous for his pearl-handled pistol. Like Hitler, Patton believed in astrology. Both men, Harry had read, based their war strategies on astrological positions of the planets and stars.

It was while he was learning to fire an O9 rifle that Harry met his first best buddy. The old-fashioned O3, by the way, is more accurate than the modern-day M-1—a favorite workhorse of U.S. WWII armies. Harry marveled at the organization and split-second timing of army training. Then there was the day when he found out that putting on a belt had to be done a special way. During a routine inspection, Harry was the only soldier with his belt inserted from the right. For that, he was "gigged" and ordered to report for KP duty rather than enjoy a weekend pass.

There was so much to do, so much to learn, so many weapons to master! No wonder General Patton observed, "War is the only thing Man does well."

In all armies of the world, soldiers work in teams of two—one man to cover the other's activities. In the service, you never do anything on your own or you risk being sent home in a body bag. Hemingway got it right when he supposedly said, "A man alone ain't got no chance."

Harry's first partner, Roy Renard, was a light-skinned Afro-Bahamian-Haitian. His buff body was the barracks shower room epitome of virility. Roy was bucking for U.S. citizenship attainable by serving in the military. Roy, like most West Indians, had a touch of the tar brush, as they once said about Negro genes. He passed for white and occasionally presented himself as Spanish. Roy's ancestry apparently had set him up a natural-born entertainer with a great sense of rhythm and a talent for modern dance. Roy hoped one day to become a rich and famous entertainer. But for now, Harry and Roy competed for the best score in firing a rifle. There were three degrees of rifle expertise—marksman, sharpshooter, and expert. A badge that looked much like the German Iron Cross went with the high score attainable by avoiding Maggie's Drawers. That was the name for the red flag that waved across the target board when a gunner trainee failed to hit any point on the target board.

The legendary BAR—or Browning Automatic Rifle—could kill the most men in the least amount of time, as could the .50-caliber machine gun. When James Jones's angel Lowney Handy was reading prepublication *From Here to Eternity* copy, she thought BAR was a saloon and wanted the word restyled as Bar.

Harry's weapon of choice was the lightweight carbine, which he could strap, with minimum discomfort, over his left shoulder. Being of frugal "Depression kid" nature, he admired the affordable grease gun—so named because it resembled the tool mechanics used to grease automotive parts. Although notoriously inaccurate, the so-called grease gun pulled his firepower way to the right. The grease gun, however, could be manufactured for a mere nine dollars.

Then there was the ultimate death machine known as a bazooka. This heavy weapon took two men to load it and a single firing to blow up a tank.

Harry dreaded poison-gas sessions. That required entering a room slowly filling with tear gas. After a few whiffs of sinus-searing gas, he put on a gas mask, offering protection from any more toxic fumes. Poison gas had been used in World War I and had caused U.S. Doughboys to suffocate. They also coughed up bits of their lungs as bloody clots. Poison-gas warfare considered so inhumane that there was a postwar ban against it. Most World War II GIs were convinced that the WWI rule was for real. So they threw away their gas masks and instead used the containers for food, cigarettes, chocolate, and whatever else took their fancy.

Just before rifle inspection, Harry stripped and cleaned his M-1 as quickly as possible. Just one speck of dust in the barrel of his "piece," and he would "get gigged." That could mean KP, an order to "drop to the floor, soldier, and do fifteen push-ups, no, make that twenty" or a "GI party." That meant scrubbing the barracks floor with a brush and some of the foulest-smelling soap in all Christendom. Punishment for just one bit of dust in a rifle barrel fell in the category of "chicken s—t." Read that as the s-word that Sunday school-trained Harry was too shy to use.

Speaking of s—t, most GIs spiced nightly "bull sessions" with low-class street language. The f-word became a noun, verb, adverb, and/or adjective to describe just about everything. Harry's religious training proclaimed that use of such language would result in the order: "Go wash your tongue with soap and water."

Among orientation sessions was one that had to do with proper conduct as a POW—or prisoner of war. Everyone understood that they were honor bound to try and escape. If caught, they knew that the Articles of War permitted their execution by firing squad. A PW was required to give his name, rank, and serial number and nothing more. Serial numbers provided quite a bit of personal information. For example, Harry's number started with a 3, meaning he was a draftee and not a volunteer. A number 5 revealed residency in the U.S. Fifth District, which included his native Ohio.

Of all army maneuvers, he thought bivouac—also called *bushwhack*—was as good as it got. He liked nothing better than to pitch a pup tent in a woodsy Signal Corps campsite nestled in the Ozark Mountains. As a little boy, he wanted to be a rich-kid Boy Scout and go camping with the more privileged kids in Ottawa Hills—the most rural and picturesque of Toledo's more prosperous suburbs. When it came to break time, however, there was a non-Boy Scout beverage—namely, strong black "caffeine fixes" of coffee. Harry didn't take to the bitter taste of coffee routinely poured into his canteen cup. But he pretended to like it anyway. After all, coffee was America's favorite fuel—second only to oil as the world's most valuable commodity.

The words of marching songs also would have been unwelcome in Boy Scout circles, what with tunes like

> You had a good home and you left.
> Your left, your right, left, right, left, right, sound off!
> You're not behind the plough,
> You're in the army now,
> You'll never get rich,
> You son of a b—ch,
> You're in the army now.

Nighttime drinking songs were a little more "spicy," as Florrie would say whenever she sent her number 1 son to the bookmobile to select her notion of "spicy" reading matter. Later, in the armed forces, songs provided spiciness to spare—X-rated tunes like "Dirty Gertie from Bizerte" and the ever popular "Bang Bang Lulu":

Lulu had a boyfriend,
She fed him caster oil,
And everywhere that Lulu went,
Her boyfriend had to go.
Rich girls use [brand name deleted],
Poor girls use a rag,
But Lulu's is so big and round,
She stuffs in burlap bags.

On weekends, there were dancing, smoking, and drinking at the Red Cross Canteen—and there were women, as well as polite conversations. Otherwise, Harry found out, men without women used four-letter words like they were going out of style.

Meanwhile, back at the canteen, GIs adept at boogie-woogie made the biggest hit with young women recruited to "swing and sway with Sammy Kaye" records during Saturday night canteen dances. Among the most popular vocalists were the Andrews Sisters, famous for their jazzy rendering of "Boogie woogie bugle boy of Company B." The Andrews trio was the first Jewish musical group to send a Yiddish title—"Bei Mir Bist du Schon"—to the top of the charts. Another jitterbug hit of Harry's service time was "Man alive! I got the GI jive." Dysentery, a common ailment in the service, led to editing along lines of "Man alive. I got the GI s—s!"

Other songs were equally flavored in dark humor, for example, "Good-bye Mama, I'm Off to Yokahama"; "You Can Keep Your Knittin' and Your Purlin', If I'm Agonna Go to Berlin, Gimme a Girl in My Arms Tonight"; "Praise the Lord and Pass the Ammunition."

Meanwhile, back on the rifle range, Roy scored as an "expert" rifleman by one point. Harry won mere sharpshooter status—also by one point. Those rifle scores led to reassignment—to the infantry. So the two friends were assigned six weeks "retread" training at Camp Livingstone, outside Alexandria, Louisiana. It was in the pinewoods of Central Louisiana that Generals Dwight Eisenhower, George Marshall, and George Patton staged war games as training for the expected invasion of Hitler's fortress Europe.

All too soon, it was wintertime, complete with below-zero temperatures back home in Ohio. But in Louisiana, the November/December warmth and the refreshing scent of Louisiana pine forests made Harry resolve to live in a warm climate if he survived the war. His dream was fortified by the way leisurely life in the Deep South had became the number 1 subject in letters to and from the home front.

"Hey," said one of Harry's colleagues right after opening a letter postmarked in the Deep South, "get a load of this. My grandma wants to know 'do the darkies still sit on the plantation steps and strum their banjoes and sing all night?'"

Harry was upset by the word "darkies," uttered within earshot of his buddy Roy. As the outfit's only soldier of Negro extraction, Roy had to do everything just right. Otherwise, bigot tongues would wag and liberals would gag.

Along about Christmastime, six weeks of "retread" training made combat-ready infantrymen out of former Signal Corpsman Harry Bandera. Meanwhile, German warriors had killed 19,000 and wounded 80,000 Americans in the Ardennes forest pre-Christmas campaign known as the Battle of the Bulge. Whole towns in Belgium were destroyed. Hitler's idea was to recapture Antwerp, push the Allies back to England, and subsequently win the war. Against the advice of his military commanders, Hitler ordered a foray into the weakest link of the Ardennes forest defense lines.

On December 16, 1944, that Panzer—or Panther—tanks rolled forward into eastern Belgium. Among the first to tally heavy losses were infantrymen of the 106th Division. A roaring lion served as the division's shoulder patch. However, the lion was no match for the Nazi panther. The constant shelling and killing left the pre-Christmas snows splattered with the blood and gore of some of the Allies' finest, healthiest young men.

Anti-German sentiment hit a new high after SS troops killed—execution style—some ninety U.S. war prisoners at Malmédy, Belgium. The totally unprepared U.S. 106th Division, with their lion shoulder patches on proud display, subsequently surrendered to Nazi Germany's finest storm troopers. Little did Harry know that he would soon be wearing the 106th Division shoulder patch issued to replacements for GIs killed and disabled in the Belgian Bulge.

During fierce fighting in the snowy Ardennes, Germans captured 7,000 prisoners of war. Many wore the red keystone shoulder patch symbolizing the Pennsylvania Keystone Twenty-eighth Division. The patch was cartooned by the Nazis as a bucket spilling out blood—hence the nickname Bloody Bucket Division. The bloody bucket, instead of being derisive, became a badge of honor for Pennsylvania GIs.

Harry spent most of his spare time reading war news streaming from places like Allied Supreme Headquarters, Berlin, and Bavarian hangouts of Adolf Hitler. Some, if not most, news was top secret. So Harry had to be content with whatever censors wanted to release to the general public. Only superficial details appeared in the army newspaper *Stars and Stripes*, nicknamed the *Scars and Gripes*. However, it eventually became common knowledge that the Germans, with half a million men fighting in the Bulge, suffered more than 100,000 casualties and lost 800 irreplaceable tanks. The United States, with 600,000 troops, counted 80,000 casualties, including 15,000 captured and 19,000 killed. This called for such unusual acts as Supreme Headquarters Dwight "Ike" Eisenhower's order that Negroes would be eligible for frontline combat—a first in the annals of World War II history. The Nazis sent teenage and preteen boys into frontline action. And so the United States sent more and more U.S. teenagers to front lines. That's where Harry and his teenage buddy Roy came into the picture because so many teenagers were sent on one-way trips to faraway battlefields all over the globe.

What probably saved Harry's life was a mothers' march on Washington, D.C. All of a sudden, mothers of dead and injured teenage soldiers raised a ruckus. They protested sending poorly trained youngsters to fight the highly professional Nazi war machine. German troops, according to General Patton, were "the world's finest fighting men."

After boot camp, Harry scored a furlough to see his family in Ohio. Then he took off for training in night fighting, bayonet stabbing, firing of .50-caliber machine guns, and other war matters at Fort Meade, Maryland, near Washington, D.C. He was uncomfortable about jabbing a bayonet into a mattress serving as a virtual Japanese soldier. The blade had to be thrust just so, then it was thrust upward and sideways in order to disembowel the enemy. Did this training mean he was going to have to fight the Japanese? This he didn't want. He considered European service to be less dangerous.

As luck would have, he had relatives near Fort Meade—Uncle Arlie and Aunt Minnie Dicke of Arlington, Virginia. Arlie worked at the Pentagon. He and Minnie invited Harry to spend springtime, weekend passes in the nation's capital. He saw both the single and double cherry blossoms on trees presented long ago by Imperial Japan—once a friend, but now America's archenemy.

Once or twice, Uncle Arlie took Harry to the Pentagon—where Private Harry nearly wore out his right arm. That was the appendage constantly being raised in salutes to the multitude of high-ranking officers with business at the Pentagon.

Fort Meade training for night fighting provided such tips as "stand perfectly still whenever a flare goes off. They are more apt to see you and shoot at you if you move around." To this day, he practiced this bit of advice about protection from nighttime attacks.

Few took Fort Meade training seriously, what would you expect of a company comprising teenagers? At night, he and his buddies would have an impromptu jazz session after lights-out. Officers in charge were lenient, referring to their group as the Problem Children and overlooked out-of-control parties after the order for "lights-out." Officers in charge saw the youngsters as cannon fodder, "so let them have some fun before the Germans blast them to kingdom come." It became a case of gladiator-style "eat, drink, and be merry, for tomorrow we die."

One of Harry's most unprofessional maneuvers involved mock invasions during the night. For one thing, he wouldn't stand still when flares were fired. Move around and you would be a likely target. To teenagers, night combat training was like a jolly game of tag complete with the rockets' red glare, bombards bursting in air—just one great big game more expensive and extravagant than anything in civilian life.

At times, there would be announcements such as "We're dead. We're all dead." That happened whenever pretend spies were "killed" by means of a shoulder tap. If and when Harry came across an invading spy, he was supposed to tap the intruder on the shoulder and then report the individual as dead. On one occasion, as Harry was entering "enemy" territory, a Mexican American tapped him on the shoulder and said, "Shhhhhhhhh." At that point, both teenagers "invaded" each other's territories. The Mexican American trainee reported seeing "a Japanese on a bicycle and yelling in accented English, 'Peanoots! Popcorn! Soda pop!'"

On April 12, 1945, Harry and fellow trainees boarded a train going from Fort Meade to Camp Myles Standish near Taunton, Massachusetts. This was to be one of the saddest trips of Harry's life—not because of the war, but because a stroke had just killed President Roosevelt. Several GIs shed tears when their train passed the Massachusetts State Capitol and saw it draped in black. It made it all the more clear that the nation had lost its president and commander in chief.

Harry S Truman was now the new president. The S, by the way, stood for nothing. The president's parents disagreed on a middle name in honor of two favorite family members. Both had names beginning with S. So a plain S was a compromise. Purists go for the S without a period, hence Harry S Truman.

Aside from President Roosevelt's demise, there was another tragic death during Harry's three-week teenager Problem Children session at Camp Myles Standish. That was the April 18, 1945, sniper shooting of syndicated newspaper columnist Ernie Pyle. Pyle was Harry's idea of the perfect reporter when it came to describing the lives of an ordinary citizen soldier—an average "GI Joe from Kokomo." Pyle's reporting was chockablock with colorful, yet plain, tell-it-like-it-is American English.

On a lighter note, he scored a day pass to see Boston. Most of his friends headed for the red-light district Scollay Square. Harry was so naive he got lost trying to find the bus stop at Pack Square. He had failed to understand that "Park Square" in Bostonian dialect came out as "Pack Square." Harry stopped to have his shoes shined and was asked, "Where are you headed, soldier?" Harry hemmed and hawed, and suddenly, the man shining Harry's shoes caught on. "Sorry," he apologized, "I understand." What he understood was this: a troopship was dockside at Boston harbor's Atlantic Pier and headed for a top secret destination, so mum was the word.

The first few days at sea were uneventful—even boring. Since there was no convoy protection, the lone ship took a zigzag course across the Atlantic in a trip that was to take ten days from Boston to France. The men played cards, gambled, talked about women they left behind, discussed their postwar dreams, and then talked some more about women, and then more women, and still more women. A day or so from Gibraltar, the former luxury liner SS *Mariposa* was met by British Royal Navy ships. They provided protection for the rest of the long sea voyage to the hell of war. By this time, Harry and colleagues had figured out, to their delight, that they were headed for Europe. This was much more preferable than Pacific duty.

On April 29, 1945, Harry learned that American troops had liberated a German concentration camp at a place called Dachau. The Americans saw freight trains piled high with skin-and-bone cadavers. Blood and gore glistened on some of the railroad tracks. It proved that the Nazis machine-gunned anyone attempting to escape. Harry also learned about ceiling-high stacks of murder victims in death factories such as Auschwitz-Birkenau, Buchenwald, and Ravensbrück. There was a total of 22 death camps, plus 165 work camps. Camp entrance gates noted in German *Arbeit Machs Frei* (Work Makes You Free). Ironically, the death camps provided primarily Jewish labor for IG Farbenindustrie AG—producer of Zyklon B. The latter is a cyanide gas used to kill more than three million Jews. Some seven million people were sent to concentration camps, and only half a million survived.

On April 29, 1945, reliable sources indicated that Harry's ship was going to dock in either French North Africa or the south of France. On that sunny spring day, the *Mariposa* was greeted by Royal Navy warships sent out of Gibraltar. Roy was so happy he almost cried. Why? He now realized he would soon be in the land of his ancestors on the French Haitian side of the family blanket. Roy couldn't wait to show Harry his prized book stuffed in the bottom of his duffle bag. "My mom gave me this, and it's going to be a hell of a big help." At that point, Roy shared a beat-up paperback entitled *La Belle France* and subtitled *Its Fine Food and Wonderful Wines.*

"Well," said Harry, "looks like we are going to dine in style. No more SOS. Instead of s—t on a shingle, looks like it'll be snails and frog legs."

"Don't sweat it," said Roy. "Frog meat tastes like chicken. And you better know what chicken tastes like. You ate enough poultry back on the farm—it's a wonder you ain't grown feathers."

The news of April 30, 1945, turned the ship into Party Central. Every man aboard the "slow boat to hell" cheered, yelled, and laughed as if the war had ended, which maybe it had. It had just been revealed that Hitler and staff had taken their own lives in a Berlin bunker. First to be killed were Hitler's dogs, including his beloved German shepherd Blondi. Hitler's secretaries were issued poison capsules—along with an apology for not giving better good-bye gifts.

On the afternoon of April 30, 1945, Hitler and his bride—the former Eva Braun—killed themselves. So did Propaganda Minister Dr. Josef Goebbels and his wife. Their six children also were put to death. Then all the corpses were cremated—but not before Hitler radio signaled Admiral Karl Dönitz that he was Hitler's successor. In the grand finale, the Führerbunker was set afire—just after some 500 surviving occupants had taken to the streets. They hoped not to become one of some 100,000 prisoners taken by the Russians in their successful conclusion of the Fall of Berlin.

But for Harry, the war was just beginning, not ending. On May 1, 1945, it was announced over the loudspeaker that the *Mariposa* was about to dock in Marseille, France. The harbor's fortress-prison-torture chamber Château d'If was pointed out as the island "Alcatraz" of the fictional *Count of Monte Cristo.*

"I guess you know," said Harry, "*The Count of Monte Cristo* was written by a Negro."

"Yeah, sure," Roy said, "we darkies aren't as dumb as we look. Right?"

With a glint of mischief in his eyes, Harry couldn't resist answering, "Yeah. Right. You're *dumber* than you look."

As the ship docked, there was a frisky welcome from young and not-so-young women gathering by the score at Marseille's main pier. Just about every "working girl" in town began yelling and blowing kisses at the thousands of GIs who hadn't seen a woman in at least ten days and nights. Gloriously happy, GIs responded by removing condoms from prophylactic kits otherwise filled with sulfa drugs. The condoms, all of a sudden, were blown up into balloons and tossed dockside to the delight of women looking forward to meeting and entertaining hundreds of handsome young Yankees.

However, the officer of the day was not amused. He began shouting over the ship's public address system something about "Misuse of government property will cease immediately or before—or you will all face a court martial." It was no military secret as to what that meant—a quick trial and then off to the brig or more than likely—a dishonorable discharge.

Order was restored within minutes, and happy hookers were replaced by American Red Cross hostesses. They sold coffee, donuts, and even shaving kits—all at an affordable price—but some of the guys thought it should be gratis.

Eventually, it was time for the soldiers to climb aboard trucks and adopt a "let's roll" mode as they took off amidst out-of-control cheering and gifts of flowers and red wine. At the end of the ride, the young men set up pup-tent accommodations for an overnight stay at a "repple-depple"—or troop replacement depot.

(Many years later, Harry was to meet Marseille repple-depple veterans at an American Legion/French Consulate party to award a French ministry of defense *diplome* to Allied participants in France's liberation from D-day 1944 to VE Day 1945.)

Legalized prostitution was only the first of many culture shocks as Harry traveled through Europe, especially France. As for his English sojourn, he rated "compassionate leave"—the special passes and ration coupons for soldiers who had relatives in Europe. Actually, Harry had relatives in Germany, and this information was best kept a secret because any soldier in danger of shooting his relatives was subject to a Far East assignment. Why German relatives? Well, Florrie's favorite cousin Eric Yeomans had served his British king and country in what was called the Great War to End All Wars. He was sent to Germany where he fell in love and married Beatty, an Anglo-German beauty. The couple then established a cutlery factory in the Ruhr's industrial city of Solingen.

It all goes to show that war works in mysterious ways. During World War I, Germany's Kaiser Bill and cousin King of England exchanged Christmas cards while their subjects shot, bayoneted, bombed, gassed, and maimed each other.

2

War Sucks

A mad captain with an imperial ego could incorporate the world, become the world, consume the world, and bring everything down to destruction.

—Gavan Daws, *A Dream of Islands* (1980)

On May 1, 1945, Harry arrived in the subtropical French Riviera. He wrongly assumed that the Riviera would be warm and sunny. He thought there was no need to unpack and/or go to sleep under a cozy, warm woolen blanket. Right? Wrong! He spent his first night in Europe as a flash-frozen, sleep-deprived, stressed-out GI.

Just after reveille on May 2, he was trucked to a railroad rendezvous several kilometers north of Marseille.

So this was it. It would soon be a time to kill or be killed.

"Wow!" Harry thought when he saw the long row of dilapidated railroad cars. It was happening all over again. Harry suddenly recalled stories that his father had served in France during World War I. He wondered, then, "Did my father also go to war courtesy of transportation by a 40 et 8?"

He also remembered being told that his father had been gassed in World War I and wasn't "right in the head," this being grounds for a divorce and for never mentioning his name. All of Harry's inquiries about his father were quickly put down. He didn't know anything about his father's European roots. Once, after a few minutes of pestering, Florrie cut off her son with "Oh, I don't know, he was Hungarian or something."

For many years, Harry thought he was part Hungarian. And then he found a letter hidden in a laundry basket. On the letter was the return address of his father's sister. So Harry wrote and discovered that his father was of Polish descent and carried the surname Slusarczyk-Salin. He also learned that his father had served in France during World War I. Rather than seek more details about his roots, Harry decided to leave well enough alone. After all, it must be tough to raise another man's son as your own, and Harry was thankful to the Flagg family for having done a fine job of taking care of him.

There was no time to think about incidents that happened years ago. Number 1 priority was to climb aboard a freight car, preferably one of the newer ones. Harry thought about choosing a 40 et 8 on the chance he might be repeating his father's World War I experiences. He quickly changed his mind and ran as fast as he could to a coach more apt to be of recent manufacture. Luckily, both he and his buddy Roy got aboard a coach cleaner and newer than most of the others.

After many rail and engine repairs and seemingly endless stop-and-go travel, the train traveled many miles away from the hills overlooking Marseille—capital of Provence. As it did, Harry had a front-row seat to view hills and meadows of golden ripening wheat made all the more beautiful by hundreds of bright red poppy blossoms. The poppies made him think of "Flanders fields where poppies grow" among graves of World War I GIs—or Doughboys as American soldiers were nicknamed at that time. All of a sudden, Harry mused that dead soldiers make good fertilizer, thereby making France the biggest food exporter in Western Europe.

It wasn't the crops that made the deepest impression. It was the young mostly pretty French women who scored the most attention. The trainload of GIs moved so slowly that it was possible to do a little socializing.

"Hey, Frenchy," a GI hollered at Roy, "you can parley-*vous*. Right? So talk to the pretty lady."

Roy obliged by calling out, "Bonjour, mademoiselle. Comment allez-vous?" The woman pedestrian smiled and said in perfect English, "I'm fine. How are you?"

Harry was "over the moon" about seeing Provence with its ancient sunbaked hilltop villages and quiet tree-lined country roads. What he saw even smelled better than Ohio. Rising out of the terra-cotta-hued soil were fields of lavender—Florrie's favorite scent. Lavender scents were aided and abetted by fragrant rosemary and thyme.

And then there was the matter of Harry's newly discovered sin—the imbibing of strong drink. As many Ohio churchgoing women had warned, "Lips that taste wine will never taste mine."

Out came a guidebook, and Harry read about "delicious, full-bodied reds, fruity roses, dry and bubbly whites, and sweet fortified wines . . . perfect for dishes drenched in garlic and olive oil, *bouillabaisse* made from all kinds of seafood, *rouille* or red pepper and garlic sauce, *ratatouille* stew of peppers, onions, eggplant, and squash—as well as *pissaladière* or onion tart, followed by melt-in-the-mouth almond cookies."

It was now time for his lips to taste wine. "Know what?" said Harry. "If I get out of this alive, I am going to make French vino my favorite sin. I want to know everything I can about wine, and to hell with the church thing against the so-called sin of drinking. Heck, when Jesus attended a wedding, he made wine, not water. That has to tell you something."

His perceived Gallic penchant for art made Harry vow to learn more about All Things French. Early on, Harry had a knack for drawing and painting. He did some serious detective work and found out that his father also had artistic talent. So it was in his genes for him to know that near-perfect Provence lighting was a painter's wet dream. He understood why so many master artists had painted scenes Harry was now admiring—people like Van Gogh, Cézanne, Matisse, Picasso, and Harry's favorite Paul Gauguin.

In due time, he tired of endless olive groves and vineyards. He just wanted to get some sleep. After all, he was just a growing boy, and he needed more rest than the older men. His elders could therefore enjoy the scenery while he did what some teenagers do best—sleep. The railroad car was so crowded that the GIs had to grab their forty winks in shifts. By some sort of unspoken *camaraderie*, the older men relinquished part of their rest shifts to youngsters like Harry and Roy.

It seemed to take forever as the beat-up train passed through Alsace with its seventeenth-century half-timber houses along cobblestone streets radiating from a central fountain. There was occasional bartering for the famous wines of Alsace. Oddly enough, no money passed hands. French franc notes were supersized and printed in pretty colors on what seemed like a cross between toilet tissue and wallpaper. It required thousands of francs for even a small purchase. The United States, in cooperation with French authorities, issued occupation script. These colorful minibills were of little value, so cigarettes were the currency of the day. And if you had a pair of nylons, all Europe would be at your feet. You could have anything you needed plus anything you wanted.

A couple of days after leaving the south of France, the train pulled into Strasbourg—fourth largest city in the Texas-sized republic of France. The city was chockablock with sturdy stone and timber buildings as romantic as they were masterpieces of architectural and engineering splendor.

For centuries, Strasbourg had been under, first, German and then French jurisdiction. Harry noticed that saying "Strahz-boor" indicated pro-French sympathies. If the word came out "Strahs-burg," well, that could mean a preference for German occupation.

According to Harry's GI guidebook, Strasburg and its Alsatian surroundings "might look German, but they aren't. Until 1697, when the region became French, Alsace was a confederation of independent cities, some heavily Germanic."

Frequent Franco-German warfare led to such rhetoric as the English restyling German Alsatian shepherd dogs as *Alsatian*, thereby dropping German connections. The French, too, had joined the canine name game. Their national dog, closely related to the German war dog called a Pudle Hund or puddle hound—the pooch loved water—was Gallicized as a *caniche*. The English and Americans preferred the name poodle for their scaled-down, man-made version of the much larger, fiercer German Pudle Hund.

Roy's book said the troops should expect to see in Alsace "dense evergreen forests spread up the mountainsides above fields of thickly planted vine rows."

As for the wines, there would be glasses of the local gewürztraminer to wash down stick-to-the-rib courses heavy on meats and sauerkraut. But that was to come later when the war was over, and Harry got to explore Alsace in a more casual manner. For now, he was content with half-timbered buildings bedecked with geraniums and sporting wrought-iron signs advertising the profession of current or past occupants. Most of the social life was based at the local *winstub*—a wine bar/restaurant/tavern. Or so Roy's "magic book" indicated.

Harry couldn't get enough information about his newly discovered "sin"—the consumption of wicked drinks like wine. "Know what?" he said to Roy. "Quick as I get out of the army, I'll read up on wines. I want to know all about the hundreds of different wines from the most expensive fruit on earth—the grape. Just think. A few grapes can come up with a hundred-dollar wine just like that! And where I come from—Ohio—there are plenty of grapes and a connection with France since Ohio was once part of New France, the colonial jewel of Old France."

"Oh, man alive," Roy said. "Has my mom's book created a monster? A wino? That won't set too well with the folks back home in that uptight little church you had to attend."

"If this be treason, then make the most of it," Harry said.

The next thing Harry remembered were the acres upon acres of hillside vineyards as the train slowly made its way north to Strasbourg.

All of a sudden, the death and destruction of war became an obsession. Harry realized that his days were numbered because he was so much closer to possible or probable death and injury in the killing fields of Europe. His vulnerability became even more real when the French train broke down next to a hamlet where there had been recent tank combat. Every house lay in ruins with their roofs on the floor and floors shoved skyward like some bizarre creation of a mad architect. Tank tracks churned surrounding fields into muddy puddles. One of the tanks didn't make it. The tank's cockpit lid had been lifted, and a grenade dropped inside. It could be assumed that there were no survivors.

So this was it. Harry was about to experience close encounters of the war kind.

With that thought in mind, a short stroll ended in a chapel with nothing intact except a fire-charred cross on a bullet-splattered altar. Harry dropped to his knees, pressed his hands in prayer mode, and sought to talk with a Higher Power:

> Hello, God. It's me. I'm in trouble again. Sorry to pray mostly when I need help. Forgive, please. I guess you know I am scared out of my cotton-pickin' mind. I never thought it would come to kill or be killed. I doubt I will come out of this alive if I ever have to fight with probably the best soldiers in the world—namely, the Germans. After all, their belt buckles say *Gott Mit Uns*—or God Is with Us. All the time, I hear you are on our side, not theirs. And please don't let me be the last American killed in World War II. I want just a little taste of combat duty. War makes the best raw material for the best tall tales. Right? It's been that way from Homer to Hemingway. If it's okay with you, please get me through this mess, all in one piece and with some good war stories to write and talk about. I don't know what I can do in return. But I will think of something. Maybe you will too, so I'm all ears, send me a message or sign, okay? Please, God, this isn't much of a prayer, and I am being selfish, and I am taking up too much of your time. You must be really busy these days. Uh-oh, I see the guys loading up on the world's slowest train. They must have fixed it and the tracks again for the umpteenth time. I gotta go. Amen.

He got up off his knees and crossed himself. He wasn't Catholic. It just seemed to be the right thing to do. He took a last look at the ruined chapel and then ran to the train about to take off one more time. He felt much better after his talk with God. For the first time since shipping out from Boston, he believed he might actually come out of this mess alive—maybe even without a scratch. Just at the moment, though, he had to "go when you gotta go"; so he was more concerned about train station sanitation rather than death and dismemberment. Railroad restrooms were limited to a hole in a concrete floor. You had to squat over the hole just so, feet firmly implanted in a metal footprint, and then it was a matter of "bombs away."

At long last, the train crossed into war-torn Germany, and as the saying goes, "The cheese became more binding." This is it, Yankee soldier, you are now in a position to hear shots fired in anger.

Aside from thoughts of death and destruction, Harry marveled at the contrast in demographics. France seemed almost devoid of children, but in Germany, there were kids everywhere. Sooner or later, one of the little streetwise youngsters would attach himself to a soldier and beg for chewing gum, cigarettes, or chocolate bars in return for such treasures as "You want my mother? She virgin!"

As the train clicked and clacked toward the industrial Saar, the weather became nasty as hell. Dark clouds poured sheets of heavy rain that churned fields into a sea of sloppy mud.

"When those cannons blast off," Roy said, "and shells blow up, lightning flashes and the thunder and noise make it rain like hell. No wonder we are in mud up to our belly buttons."

The sky was pitch-black when the train chugged into a smoky, dirty Saarland terminal. It was here that the troops were to transfer to another train headed deeper inside the Third Reich. Before boarding, just few feet away, a jeep splashed mud on the khaki pants of a tall blond soldier with big glowing milky-blue eyes. The GI pulled out a handkerchief, took a swipe over his muddy trousers, and cussed, "Kiss my homesick a—."

"Never fear," said Harry, "sad-sack me is here, in the service and at your service." He reached inside a duffle bag and pulled out a tabloid newspaper—official publication of the U.S. Army.

"Hey," Harry said, "soak down the *Scars and Gripes* and have a good GI scrub down."

"Thanks, buddy," said the GI with the goofy grin and mud-splattered combat boots. Harry operated solo for the moment, so he was looking for a partner, preferably someone his own age. He was aware that in the army, as in police departments, no one worked alone. Two heads are better than one. It is always best to look out for each other and especially to cover each other's movements to different positions.

Harry approved of his prospective partner's style. Instead of tucking his pants into his combat boot tops, the guy tied a rubber around the tops and then tucked his trouser bottoms under the condom. It wasn't Army Regulation to be done in that manner, but it made for a "neater than grits" appearance. As soon as Harry's prospective buddy had wiped most of the mud off his boots, he stretched out his hand and introduced himself, "Hi. My name's Kevin. Kevin LaVern. I come from La Crosse, Wisconsin. Ever heard of it?"

Harry thrust out his hand. "Nope," he said. "But then you never heard of my hick town Berkey, Ohio. So we're both in the dark. Anyhow, it's nice to meet you. I'm Harry. Harry Bandera. Never heard of La Crosse, but I heard of Wisconsin. I was born in Milwaukee but raised in backwoods Ohio, like near Berkey, with our farm's rural free delivery route 1 address. Nearest sign of any civilization was Toledo, where they make all those Jeeps like the ones you see over here. My stepdad works at the Willys-Overland plant and inspects Jeeps, so he's proud to be part of the war effort just like us."

From there on, the two men chatted and joked and bonded in high old army-buddy mode. Harry reckoned Kevin and he were going to make a good team. Together they could take on the Krauts, Japanese, and whoever else fired shots in anger.

Harry thought it was especially great to meet someone "normal." Kevin had no Bohemian off-the-wall yearnings for world travel, fame, and fortune. That was more Harry and Roy's style. Kevin seemed like the average decent American GI Joe out to serve his country and subsequently go back to marriage, make an honest living, and provide a comfortable home for his happy family. In short, Kevin mirrored the young men that Tom Brokaw wrote about in his postwar best seller *The Greatest Generation*.

All too soon, Harry and Kevin climbed back on the troop train rolling east into the heart of industrial Germany. Next stop was to put the soldiers under a giant tent near the ancient cathedral city of Worms—famous for its liebfraumilch wine. What a nice name, it suggests a woman's milk, but the name comes from an ancient Worms nunnery dedicated to the Virgin Mary. The name Worms must sound better in German than in English, Harry thought. Once it came time to bed down, he and colleagues were warned of a possible guerrilla or Luftwaffe attack. Kevin refused to take off his shoes that night. He said he was going to "run like hell straight for the woods if any Kraut starts some fireworks."

As it turned out, a cot in a tent was more comfortable than what came next—a trenchlike ditch under a sky splattered with bullets and shells from drunken artillerymen. After the men were rousted from their "canvas city," they moved on to a field artillery unit, again near Worms. That was where Harry and colleagues were to spend the night in a ditch because no other arrangements had been made. Everyone was in a festive mood because on May 7, the Germans surrendered unconditionally. The next day was declared VE Day or Victory in Europe Day. The evening of May 8 was made festive—and dangerous—by the indiscriminate firing of various weapons of serious destruction. The racket was accentuated by the occasional explosion of .55-caliber shells from cannons with names like Belching Bitch or Bait 88. The latter showed respect for deadly eighty-eight-millimeter shells that had destroyed many—far too many—an American Sherman tank. Our tanks were small and no match for the huge German and/or Russian tanks.

It soon became clear that the infantrymen's stay with a field artillery unit would be short. But before leaving, there was to be a victory march through the ruins of Worms. This gig was on a volunteer basis. Almost every available GI volunteered. So there was a long, long line of armed Americans marching down the few streets that had been cleared of bomb damage. So there was Harry and colleagues, their M-1 rifles on the ready, and taking little notice of the dour expressions of the few Worms residents who watched the victory parade. Most Germans had been led to believe that Hitler would drive out the Allied invaders. Thus Germany ultimately would win the war. A German American GI mocked German victory thoughts when he surveyed the ruins of Worms—hometown of Martin Luther—and remarked in German, "Was ist los mit der Luftwaffe? Der Americanischer SweineHunds alles kaput maken." Loosely translated, he was saying, "What's the matter with our German Air Corps? The American pig dogs are destroying everything!"

After a short stay with a field artillery howitzer outfit, Harry and his two friends were transferred to a tank unit. Within weeks, the tankers went home to America, and Harry was then attached to a tank destroyer battalion. With so many changes in his outfit's categories, the buzz was "We get attached and reattached more often than [stripper] Gypsy Rose Lee's garter."

Within a fortnight, Harry's tank destroyer unit was demobilized, and most of its men went home to begin life anew as private citizens. Slowly but surely, the majority of American GIs in occupied Germany became military government policemen known as the constabulary. This unit's headgear comprised a gaudy yellow and orange helmet liner. It led to the nickname Potato Bug. The constabulary's job was to occupy and administer the American zone. Germany had been divided into four zones—one each for the United States, Russia, Britain, and France. The United States occupied the scenery section of Western Europe's strongest economy and most populated nation. The American zone comprised Germany's most breathtaking scenery—its vast forests of fir and beech, snowcapped mountains, and centuries-old half-timbered homes of Bavaria and Baden-Württemberg.

Harry liked the way that German farmers lived in small towns and left town to work the fields every morning. It was so unlike Ohio where 51 percent of the state was farmland peppered with isolated farmhouses large enough to be considered mansions. The lack of isolated farm homes gave Germany an aura of wide open spaces chockablock with cultivated land and forests. This was an unexpected vista in a land the size of Montana and populated with millions. Above all, there was always nature, fresh air, and a feeling of being in one of the world's healthiest environments. There was one special, peaceful moment etched in Harry's memory bank forever. That was when he was in a truck convoy moving by moonlight along a narrow road beside the Rhine River and its background of fir-clad foothills.

Harry's first constabulary headquarters was in Heilbronn, where he had his best-yet accommodations. He got to sleep, albeit on the floor, of a German family's mansion that had been confiscated as a military barracks. Occupants of a row of houses were given twenty-four hours to pack up and leave. That wasn't nearly enough time for housewives to pack up and leave homes where they had grown their families over a generation or so. There were many complaints to military government, and finally, the Heilbronners were given another twenty-four hours to secure their household goods. What a racket. There were few cars and even fewer trucks available to the conquered Germans. So they made their way through Heilbronn streets by means of small, medium, and large carts and even wheelbarrows.

While the housewives gathered favorite belongings and wept over the damage we had done, their men headed for the cellars. To their surprise, the kegs of wine were still intact. "Warrum?" they asked. "Why?" The GIs explained that there had been incidents of poisoned drinks. They were afraid to touch the household's wine supply. The Germans laughed and said this was silly. The Germans then proved their point by hosting a great wine tasting. Nobody died, so the wine apparently wasn't poisoned.

After settling into the comforts of German home life, it was Harry's duty to be one of many guards keeping Axis prisoners of war behind barbed wire. Most were German, but there were a few Hungarians and others who had fought the Allies. The prisoners were housed in row upon row of two-man tents. Here and there, a trench was installed for relief when nature called. Some of the more creative prisoners gathered stones, whitewashed them in lime, and created a sign that proclaimed in the German vernacular *Scheiss*.

Quite a few of the men, for whatever reason, refused to eat and became emaciated and listless. Many dropped dead, and their bodies were taken to a shed. There, the bodies were stacked like a cord of wood, and limestone was sprinkled over the corpses as a matter of sanitation. The scene was especially inhumane on a night when one of the guards got drunk on potato schnapps and fired a machine gun—splattering bullets hither and yon. When Harry asked about his guard colleague, he was told the man never existed; and in any case, he had been quickly and quietly transferred. The matter was hushed up and the case closed, never to be discussed. Actually, no one really cared. The prisoners were more or less dead meat and even available to use as servants, shoe polishers, and laundrymen. The officer of the day once told Harry the prisoners could be used "for whatever you want, you can cornhole them if you want, just bring 'em back alive." For a short time, he used a young Hungarian as a laundryman and boot polisher, but he hated the idea of being a virtual slave driver.

Harry and fellow GIs often were posted for short stays in nearby towns and villages. It was as if to let the Germans know we were everywhere and in great numbers, so "you Germans better behave like a proper conquered nation." Crailsheim, Ellwangen, and Schwäbisch Gmünd were among nearby towns where Harry did short stints of guard and military police duty. For the most part, it was boring to his creative mind. He spent most of his time putting together a photo album. As a GI colleague told him, "Years from now, if you are still alive, that album will mean a hell of a lot to you." Over the years, Harry was to find these words among the most truthful he had ever heard.

Finally, with so many men and technicians returning home, the way to a higher rank and better pay was wide open. Harry began by helping the supply sergeant in a walled-in castle with moat. There was no supply sergeant helper rank, so Harry became a noncommissioned officer, namely, an ammunition corporal. His supply duties didn't free him of guard duty. He was never to forget the dawn of August 15, 1945, when he was on guard duty at Crailsheim—a small town east of Schwäbisch Hall. All of a sudden, a *Stars and Stripes* jeep pulled up for clearance to proceed farther east.

"Have you heard the news?" the jeep driver said. Then he handed over a copy of the official army newspaper, and it had the huge headline WAR ENDS.

Harry felt especially privileged to be the first in his outfit to know the war in Europe had drawn to a close via unconditional surrender on August 14, 1945. Japan had gone the way of Nazi Germany—but only after single atomic bombs had destroyed first Hiroshima and then Nagasaki. Japan's surrender meant that Harry would have no more fear of being sent to the Pacific wars, a situation he dreaded like hell.

The end of the war meant a reorganization of military units and their responsibilities. There was an end to billeting troops in civilian housing and the beginning of refurbishing German bases for the use of American soldiers and airmen.

Yet again, Harry's unit was being broken apart by demobilization. On the last night before moving to a new base, Harry had the most frustrating duty of his entire military career. It seemed that every other soldier was saying good-bye to German girlfriends by means of an all-night orgy of drinking and bedding. Whenever Harry asked for a relief guard, he was told, "Go [expletive] yourself." So finally, Harry knocked at the door of the noncommissioned officer in charge. The "topkick" cracked open his bedroom door, and Harry got a quick peek at a young woman in bed trying to cover her nudity with a bedsheet. The sergeant wore a condom fitted with a so-called French tickler. Harry had heard about those things but didn't really believe—or maybe didn't want to believe—they existed. Harry's request for proper guard duty relief was met with "Don't worry about it. Go back and get some sleep."

Harry began to wonder how the military situation had become more and more bizarre, a tried-and-true example of malice on steroids. After all, he and fellow soldiers were sent to Europe to kill people, not sleep with them. There was something unkosher somewhere. According to all that was right and holy, American GIs were supposed to make war, not love.

To make a long story short, it was amazing that the unit ever made it to the next base of operations, what with the tank drivers drunk and their girlfriends equally soused.

Harry's newest base, and where he stayed the longest, was a riverside half-timber building in Schwäbisch Hall. Across the river were the towers and castlelike turrets of Hall's medieval fortifications. Here and there were fluffy white feather mattresses airing and sunning in a scene as romantic as it gets.

The old city was set in a fairy-tale valley of greenery and bloomery. Above town was a tier of sturdy two- and three-story half-timbered homes of medieval vintage. St. Michael's Church, with its onion-shaped spire, was set like a jewel in the center of town. The church was dedicated to Archangel St. Michael, patron saint of Schwäbisch Hall. In front of the church was a cascade of steps that made a grand setting for the staging of classic German theater such as Goethe's *Faust* and Schiller's *Bride of Messina*. Productions based on religion were especially impressive—like when night-lights focused on a cross used as the main prop for *The Mystery of the Holy Passion*. The lighted steps made for extraspecial bling in a scene where an actress portrayed Joan of Arc as she faced judges who would condemn her to death. By coincidence, Harry was treated to a Joan of Arc scene staged by Sweden's Oscar-winning actress Ingrid Bergman. She entertained U.S. troops by making appearances at army posts in between filming a Joan of Arc epic shot mostly in France.

In prewar years, Schwäbisch Hall's nighttime illuminations made a perfect backdrop for stage productions, festivals, and beer-garden blasts, especially the one internationally loved as *Oktoberfest*.

Just across from the church steps was the ornate town hall, dating to 1732 and capped with an iron grille shaped as a crown. The "German" eagle—adopted from the Roman legions who invaded Germany centuries ago—was front and center in the stately building overlooking Haalplaza. The latter provided a hillside setting for a marketplace in the town center. To the north of St. Michael's Church was a Red Cross club where Harry and army buddies could savor snacks, beers, and coffee, as well as occasional entertainment by ballet dancers and other artistes.

Although St. Michael's Church dominated the skyline, it was not the only medieval masterpiece of Christian architecture. Nearby was St. Catherine Church with the statue of a tearful St. Mary Magdalene in its holy sepulchre. Near Harry's Ohio farm home was a St. Catherine's Catholic Church in the tiny hamlet of Richfield Center. The church was supported by farmers of mainly German descent, and Harry wondered if there was any connection with the Ohio church's German namesake.

Harry spent much of his time walking down the narrow cobblestone alley just below the church. That was where he practiced high school journalistic skills by taking over a Nazi-tainted plant for the daily newspaper *Haller Tagblatt*. Publisher-owner Emil Schwend was under military government scrutiny for possible anti-U.S. opinions. So his newspaper print shop was available for Harry's Company D weekly journal *Dander Data*. Harry was undaunted by the fact that the printers spoke only German. So Harry figured they would just have to learn English. After two weeks, the printers—after many giggles—could say in English the word "headline." Harry, on the other hand, picked up first-rate barracks-bag German. He even befriended a young fraulein who taught him the German words to the popular war tune "Lili Marlene"—popular, that is, with German troops. During a Paris visit, Harry's request for "Lili Marlene" in a piano bar went over like a lead balloon.

After a month or so, Harry, tired of his newspaper enterprise, and the editor in chief left to join the *Stars and Stripes* staff. The final issue was paid for in cigarettes, as usual, and Emil Schwend gave Harry a gorgeous black-

and-white coffee-table book focused on Schwäbisch Hall. The book was so well produced that it became easy to accept that the German inventors of printing did the best work in this area of cultural achievement.

Harry and Schwend—from two opposing sides in a world war—had somehow bonded. Years later, when Harry returned to Schwäbisch Hall, Schwend was back in business, flew his own plane, and dreamed about moving to America!

With so much *Grimm's Fairy Tales* romance in the streets of Emil Schwend's Schwäbish Hall, there had to be a castle. "Let's go check it out," said Kevin, as he showed up with two borrowed bicycles.

So off they pedaled up and down meadows and hills with thousands of trees all planted in neat, straight lines—perfect examples of Teutonic efficiency and a green attitude about living in tandem with Mother Nature. Eventually a hilltop castle dominated the scene. According to Harry's book gift, Komberg Castle began its existence as a convent in 1150. That meant the building was centuries old before Christopher Columbus set sail for the New World. The castle was noted for its huge crystal chandelier and the tomb of the deeply religious Countess Suzanna of Limpurg.

Harry and Kevin hopped off their bikes and began to climb the hill leading to the castle when Harry suddenly stopped and noted, "Do you see what I see?"

Both soldiers nodded and smiled at the strapping young man sunbathing in the nude on the castle's sunny south side.

"Always heard the Europeans were into nudity, and now I know it's true," said Harry.

"Only they don't call it nude and lewd like back in the USA," Kevin said. "My ancestors called it 'naturism.' After all is said and done, we started out naked as a jaybird back in Garden of Eden days—so why not strip right down to our birthday suits?"

Years later, Harry was to read about German *Körperkultur* (physical culture). Un-self-conscious nude sunbathing was nothing new in Germany. It was part of a healthy pump-iron, no-red-meat lifestyle dating to the late nineteenth century. Even Hitler was a vegetarian.

Meanwhile, back at constabulary HQ, it wasn't always wonderful-wonderful. For the most part, it was hard work and long hours. Harry believed in "do it yourself so you'll know it's done right." But eventually, he wised up and got Kevin to help with the almost overwhelming S-4 chores and paperwork. In addition, a weekly post exchange was part of Harry and Kevin's routine. Sometimes, both men worked long into the night.

Kevin's favorite job was collecting uniforms to be sent to the town dry cleaner. The dry-cleaning business had been his career choice in Wisconsin, and Kevin wanted to reestablish himself in this venture after his discharge. Eventually, Kevin learned the supply sergeant routine sufficiently to become a tech sergeant like Harry.

For quite a long time, Harry and Kevin's stay in Schwäbisch Hall was pleasant but uneventful. And then the time came to move to a former air marshal Hermann Goering Luftwaffe barracks in Hessental, just outside the picture-postcard town of Schwäbisch Hall. Straightaway, out came a chisel, and a Nazi swastika under an eagle was chipped away. The eagle was fine and dandy, no problem, but the swastika had to go.

The new base provided an entirely military setting—devoid of civilians, other than service staff. That made it easier to avoid violating military government's nonfraternization rule, legalizing the arrest, and a fine for any GI caught speaking to a German. It was supposed to be General Eisenhower's way of punishing Hitler's superrace by putting them down as unfit for any conversing. Harry's rebel genes, courtesy of his English mom, almost immediately kicked in. He openly practiced his "barracks-bag German" every chance he got. He discovered that *kinder* (children) were the best teachers. If you made a mistake, kids quickly brought you to heel. It became a case of "If this little kid can speak German, why can't a smart man like me talk Kraut?"

So Harry befriended a German youngster and subsequently got invited to dine with the boy and his mother. They lived in a cottage high up on a picturesque plateau overlooking Schwäbisch Hall. Harry made a big hit by bringing coffee to a household that had only ersatz coffee derived from grains. Actually, Harry preferred the fake coffee. "Great," said his English-speaking German hosts, "that leaves the real thing for us. We haven't had real coffee in, it seems like, a hundred years." In return for coffee, there was a special treat for Harry—namely, fresh eggs. They were a great change from the powered-egg dishes served back at the base. Harry was well aware that eggs were rationed, and he expressed concern about causing a problem. His German friend gave a sly look and pointed to her dog Fritz. Then she said, "We listed Fritz as a person. After all, he is a member of the family, *nein?*"

For the most part, Harry found the guttural sounds of German difficult to imitate—even though he considered himself gifted at building a vocabulary of foreign words. So it was somewhat of a relief when bilingual Roy said, "Don't worry about it. German isn't a language. It's a throat disease."

Learning to speak German was not a number 1 priority, especially when you could get fined sixty-four dollars for speaking to a German. Aside from a language barrier, the main problem of the day was denazification. A cartoon in *Stars and Stripes* portrayed the situation by means of a fraulein with long blonde pigtails, in the style of German warrior maiden Brünnehilde. Ms. Veronica *Dankeshŏen*—that means "thank you" in English—liked swastikas and decorated her panties and other belongings in the now-forbidden Nazi insignia. Veronica Dankeshöen also liked her initials and displayed her VD identity with great pride. This evoked the number 2 postwar problem: venereal disease.

A few years later, Harry bought a Volkswagen or bug, as the world's most popular affordable car came to be known. The instant he saw his yellow VW, he thought of blonde Veronica and realized that she might be bad news. So the bug was named Veronica and became so popular that Harry's friends asked about Veronica's before they inquired about her master's health.

Meanwhile, back at the base in Germany, the constabulary unit's supply sergeant got his discharge papers and went home to America. Harry was then upgraded from corporal to staff sergeant in charge of S-4—the outfit's supply division. In addition to disbursing clothes, shoes, and military equipment, he also was in charge of the PX—or post exchange. Every other week, it was his job to distribute PX cartons of tax-free cigarettes plus watches, jewelry, French perfumes, Spanish silver work, silk scarves, and other luxuries. Sometimes he had to work late into the night. That made him too sleepy to answer roll call at reveille. In any case, his favorite army song was about "how I hate to get up in the morning." It recommended shooting the bugler "and then I'll get the other pup, the guy who wakes the bugler up." After a while, nobody messed with the PX man, and his name was never called out for reveille after some drill sergeant yelled just before dawn's arrival, "Fall out, soldiers. Rise and shine. Drop your c—s and grab your socks."

Harry's position as supply sergeant and PX administrator made it possible for Harry to sleep in whenever he felt so inclined. After all, anyone who crossed the supply sergeant might find his name dropped from the list of those in line for the purchase of luxury items available at the squadron PX.

So now the war was over. It was a time to celebrate. First, there was a baseball game in Nürnberg's spacious amphitheater where Hitler had made many a speech. A scratched-out swastika dominated the stadium. Nearby, Nazi leaders were being tried for war crimes. Top leader Hermann Goering escaped the gallows because he smuggled inside his cell a two-inch bottle of killer cyanide. That was all it took to cheat death by hanging. He hated the idea of death by hanging and being aware of your spinal cord snapping, and at about the same time, you soiled your trousers. A rope necklace, Goering realized, could precede a slow death comprising twenty minutes of terrible suffering. This, the Nazi leader didn't need. Harry's mind now had enough of negativity, death, diarrhea, and all the rest of it. It was time to switch to travel, get a life, and organize the traditional European Grand Tour—once a perk reserved exclusively for English gentlemen of the Victorian and Edwardian eras. Before making a trip, Harry read all the army-issued guidebooks he could get. He became a biped guidebook with tons of tips on what to see and do during furloughs and passes to German tourist centers as well as those in Paris, Brussels, Switzerland, and England.

Harry soon realized that he was king of the world, a citizen of the only world power to escape serious war damage. Factories and businesses were intact and open for business as usual. America was the only nation with so much surplus food it took millions of dollars just to store the stuff. It was the best of times to be an American and enjoy the spoils of war.

The war was NOT over for Europeans. Their gloomy postwar world brought hunger, black market, international hatred, and lots of talk about another world war—this time against Communist Russia. Even royalty suffered as, one after the other, their thrones became obsolete. Before the war, Great Britain was the strongest power on earth, and its King-Emperor reigned but did not rule over a third of the world. After history's most pricey war, there were few employed monarchs left. It was beginning to look like exiled Egyptian King Farouk had said it like it is, namely, "In future, there will be only five kings, the King of Hearts, the King of Clubs, the King of Spades, the King of Diamonds, and the King of England."

Eastern Europe got the worst end of the deal. Russians, having lost 20 million dead, took a terrible revenge. Their part of Germany was looted, the women raped, and there was brutality above and beyond the call of duty.

During checkpoint duty, Harry saw endless streams of destitute refugees, their meager possessions loaded on broken-down carts and wagons of every description. These long columns of people hailed from many countries and would do anything to get food, lose their past, get papers and passports for a new life, or, in the case of Nazis, escape to South America—especially Brazil and Argentina.

Carefree Harry had sightseeing on his mind. His first such venture concentrated on Heidelberg, with its imposing fifteenth-century castle, a Gothic-Renaissance ruin of red stone. After a tour and lunch, he took long walks in the exquisite town with Germany's oldest university, a place made immortal by its *Student Prince* heritage. Because of its beauty, Heidelberg was declared an "open city" and therefore not a target for Allied bombs. Except for the city's bridges over the Necker River, Heidelberg suffered no war damage. So Harry spent many happy hours exploring the partially ruined castle which had so intrigued Mark Twain in his best seller *Innocents Abroad*. Harry especially admired the castle cellar's beer keg so big it was topped by a dance floor. In addition, the woodlands behind the castle, the scent of pine needles, fresh cool air, and sunny summer weather were the stuff of eternal memories. He also took pleasure in the *Student Prince* legend. Why? It was because he had been editor of his Burnham High School newspaper the *Student Prints*, a play on the title for a romantic coed-and-prince tale.

The U.S. Army radio station's *Luncheon in München* show created an urge to see the area's largest city, Munich—known in German as *München*, pronounced "mern-shen" in English. All German cities were easily accessible because of the Hitler-inspired autobahn, a superhighway that provided straight-through travel throughout Germany. The system had been admired by General Eisenhower, and he eventually brought the idea to fruition in the United States.

It was part of constabulary protocol to establish speed limits on the autobahn. This made no sense to Germans. After all, the German-invented "horseless carriage" was made to travel eighty or more miles per hour, so why not do it? Thus it became Harry's job to sit in the back of the jeep and watch out for military police who would take a dim view of seventy-mile-an-hour trips to Munich—capital of the once Kingdom of Bavaria.

On the way to Munich, Harry took time out to see death camp Dachau, where there were wax models and other displays that told the true story of the Holocaust. He would never forgot the small hill filled with remains of a quarter-million Jews, homosexuals, gypsies, disabled, and whoever the Nazis wanted dead.

And so on to more positive scenes—like the Bavarian Alps and Germany's highest peak, the Zugspitze, forming a background for Garmisch-Partenkirchen and Oberammergau, site of the every-decade Passion play about the last days of Jesus. Harry had never seen such eye-popping countryside. No wonder Hitler loved it so much and established his dream home, the Eagle's Nest, in all the alpine glory of beautiful Bavaria.

But now Hitler was history. The world's bloodiest, costliest war had ended. It was time to make the most of a bad situation. So Harry spent any spare time wheeling and dealing and scheming for cheap thrills of the travel kind. The army offered three-day passes to Paris and Brussels, furloughs to the French Riviera, compassionate leave to visit European relatives, and even an opportunity to learn how to ski during a winter week in the Swiss Alps.

Harry's typing expertise made him a wiz at doing paperwork necessary to send him on trips at the expense of his world's richest uncle—Sam. There is a time for war and a time for peace, says the Bible. And for Harry, it was time to go all out for R & R—rest and recreation—in Europe's most celebrated resorts. Up to now, it was all about men who had been through hell and now wanted only to salve their wounds in the arms of a sweet, soft, loving woman. Was it any wonder, then, that these men returned home and launched the biggest baby boom in American history?

3

Peace Rocks!

And then he said one of the most interesting things I've ever heard from a tourist, even Goethe: "When we get old, what we remember are our travels."

—Thomas Swick, South Florida
Sun-Sentinel column (2006)

In September of 1945, Harry scored a pass for Paris—or Paree, as they say in French. He also snagged a pass for his Francophone buddy Roy. Within days after the paperwork, the GI buddies took off on a long, tiring train trip from Germany to the Gare de l'Est—or East Station—in Paris. The terminal was smoky, sooty, steamy, and noisy. And yet, Harry felt as if he were in a place almost sacred, with high ceilings of steel and glass that evoked the high style of an ancient cathedral. The smoke was like incense. It put him in a hypnotic spell that reeked of first-class adventure. Here was a cherished dream of seeing Paris, all within minutes of becoming a reality. For the present, however, Harry just wanted to have his first French meal, or at least a snack. He and fellow GI tourists soon got their groove back by pigging out on ham and cheese sandwiches offered by a vendor next to a ticket booth.

Back in Germany, the guys dined on such unpopular chow as K and C rations, Spam, and all-too-frequent servings of SOS. The latter was an acronym for salve on a shingle. Salve sounded more respectable than the S-word used when the guys were not within earshot of women.

For the most part, GIs respected all women. But when there were no women around, it was time to show off a misguided manliness and make fun of them. Some of the guys were not above referring to WACs—or Women's Army Corps—members as "double-breasted soldiers with built-in foxholes."

But back to arrival in the land of croissants, *croques*, and crepes—aided and abetted by the top-of-the-line wines, brandies, and liqueurs. At this special moment, all eyes focused on a blue-haired woman of a certain age. She almost immediately sold her entire stock of sandwiches artfully conceived as only a Gallic *maman* can do. Just as she had sold the last sandwich, one of the GIs started to tease for more sandwiches.

"Machine kaput?" he asked the peddler. Machine kaput meant a German female object of a GI's desire was unable to perform because of "that time of the month," venereal disease, a husband, or some other inconvenience.

To everyone's surprise, the senior Parisian answered in English, "There's nothing wrong with my machine, except she's a little old."

"So this is Paris," Harry thought. "What would be next in this City of Light, Love, and Luscious Dishes, especially the two-legged kind?" He understood that Paris had a strong sense of place. For that, some Americans hate her. Many others love her. There was seldom any opinion in between.

So far, the city had come up to his expectation of seeing stylish women with a knack for wearing silk scarves in creative ways. In front of the terminal, there seemed to be no end of flashing bare Betty Grable legs peddling bicycles down tree-lined wide boulevards of a Paris "de la." The latter words are Parisian slang referring to the many streets named boulevard *de la* this and place *de la* that.

Harry's first "de la" was the Place de la République, a short distance down the avenue de Magenta in front of the Gare de l'Est or East Station. After being loaded in the back of an army truck, he and dozens of other GIs soon arrived at one of nineteen Red Cross clubs hosting GIs slated for a well-earned postwar spree in gay Paree. Harry and Roy were assigned to bunks at the Transatlantic Club. This former palace turned Hotel Moderne faced a city square dominated by a statue much like New York's Statue of Liberty. Only this statue was dedicated to the republic which replaced the imperial monarchy of the Napoleonic era.

As soon as he had settled in, Harry ordered a fragrant fresh-baked croissant and tiny cup of coffee—even though he didn't like coffee. But, hey, this is Paris!

Upon his return to the hotel, the concierge gave Harry and Roy a map with drawings of famous landmarks to guide the way. It was the first time Harry had seen such a map. Because of the paper shortage, the map was printed on the back of a military document showing topographical details of Orleans and the Loire River valley.

"Okay," said Roy, "your first lesson is how to get around town. First we learn about the metro. I saw a station just up the street. But first, better read up on what we need to know." The map revealed such statistics as: There are 14 lines, over 86.4 miles underground and 6 miles in open air. With 348 stations, the metro could provide passage to just about anywhere in Paris or its suburbs. The map also included a section of "How to Ask Your Way" in French. Look for "sortie" when leaving the metro. To change trains, look for a yellow sign saying Correspondence. You didn't have to know French. In addition to a French name, the lines were displayed in various colors.

"Hey, man," Roy said, "this'll work. This is a good system, made-to-order for tourists. Even I, with my lousy sense of direction, can't get too lost. And if you don't know French, you can go by colors on the map. If you can't read or you're color-blind—no matter—you can go by the number of each subway line."

With that, Roy pressed a button for the city's main "de la"—Place de la Concorde. The two friends almost ran down stone steps leading to the ticket station. There was a slightly chilly breeze near the metro entrance, but once inside, the place was warm and cozy but sufficiently spacious to deter a feeling of claustrophobia down there in the bowels of Paris.

"Wow, man!" Harry said. "These steps sparkle like a thousand little diamonds. No wonder they call Paris the City of Lights, man." He was uncomfortable using the word "man" in the way mostly musicians and Negros said it.

Roy gave an Afro-Gallic shrug of his shoulders and pushed his way into the overloaded train, Harry right behind him. Once on board, there was considerable evidence of the latest fashion rage—blue or sometimes lavender hair done up in high style. Costly perfumes drenched the air.

Within minutes, a blue-tile sign proclaimed Place de la Concorde. They got off the train, walked up the steps, and were temporarily blinded by daylight made all the merrier by the sunbeams and light rain of a September Parisian morning. When the sunshine and raindrops united just so, they flashed rainbows over the basin of the biggest fountain Harry had ever seen. The fountain made the perfect centerpiece for the panoramic view all around. Here was a city obviously planned and not just put together helter-skelter like an English or American municipality. Full credit for the beauty and symmetry of Paris goes to Baron Haussmann, Second Empire city planner who launched the world's largest and costliest urban renewal project. Harry couldn't get enough of the eye-popping cityscape unfolding before him. Everything smacked of beauty and romance—the tree-lined boulevards, harmonious Haussmannian architecture, skyscraping steeples of churches, and the hilltop Arabian Nights look of Sacré Coeur Cathedral.

Like millions of other tourists—past, present, and future—Harry queued up to buy a ticket to the top of the Eiffel Tower. What a panorama of—arguably—the world's most beautiful and romantic city! It was the perfect opportunity to ponder other Parisian superlatives mentioned in various guidebooks, including those offered to GIs as an orientation course for All Things European. Here we go,

> The earth's most visited city, the world's oldest and best subway, the largest museum in the world, the most famous main drag, a nearby largest palace in the world, the most celebrated cuisine on earth, largest overseas empire after that of the British, the world's liveliest nightlife, and the globe's most famous portrait—Leonardo da Vinci's *Mona Lisa*.

Harry was by now thoroughly seduced by the scene before him. Paris, above all, was a magnet for some, if not most, of the world's most celebrated writers. Of great interest to Harry—as an American with literary ambitions—were the bookstalls along the Seine across the Notre Dame Cathedral. In his mind's eye, he could imagine Thomas Jefferson selecting books for his private collection that was to become the nucleus for the Library of Congress in Washington, D.C.

As he eyeballed eye-popping monuments in the Place de la Concorde, the first to capture his full attention was an obelisk from Egypt. This oldest man-made structure in Paris looked like a giant stone exclamation point. It was as if the obelisk was surprised at where it had found a home. In any case, the obelisk was much nicer to see than what was there before—the guillotine where Queen Marie Antoinette had her head chopped off.

For the first time, Harry found history to be alive and well and interesting beyond his wildest imagination. Back during school days, the reciting of historical dates didn't cut it. But now, he could see, feel, and even *smell* history. He began to sense the presence of long-gone celebrities. He relived French Revolution tales about decapitations of people from the king and queen on down—almost—to the Viscountess de Beauharnais. She barely escaped losing her head and went on to remarry rather well, namely, an ambitious young army corporal. He subsequently upgraded his wife's title from Viscountess to Empress of the French. Empress Josephine's descendants eventually acquired almost every European throne still in business during the early twenty-first century. It was, allegedly, Josephine's idea to style Napoléon's title as "Emperor of the French" rather than the less-democratic "Emperor of France."

All of a sudden, a large gathering of GIs from the Red Cross Transatlantic Club approached Roy, and one of them asked, "Hey, man, we couldn't help but notice you know how to talk frog. Could you help us out? We got some French gals who want to party hearty. Help us communicate, and we will make it worth your while. We got plenty cigarettes and D rations [GI chocolate bars]."

"Okay," Roy said. "You got a deal."

But Harry wasn't going.

"I can party any day. But this is my best shot at something I always wanted to do—go to the Eiffel Tower and orient myself on the general layout of this burg. That way, I'm not so apt to get lost. So you go along with the guys and tell me all about it back in the hotel, okay?"

Harry strolled past the American embassy and other former palaces, some of them restored as luxury hotels and, once again, fit for royalty. He subsequently entered a wide tree-lined park behind a bullet-scared monument to the city of Strasbourg. According to his map, the forested park was near the French White House—palace of Gallic presidents. Once again, it was a French woman who had made her mark on history. That is to say, a royal mistress had once lived and partied at the Palais de l'Elysée. The entrance to the Champs-Elysées was more rural than urban. So former farm boy Harry felt at home amongst trees and flowers in a place named after the legendary Elysian Fields of heaven.

His reverie in gay Paree was put on hold after he spotted a slim young woman dressed in classic basic black with pearls. A brightly colored silk scarf was tied in high French style around her waist. And she was looking straight at Harry's crotch! Then she murmured something he had never heard before—an invitation to go into the bushes and do things his Sunday school teachers—as well as Florrie—had forbidden. Next, there was a far more shocking offer, a no-no condemned back home as a perverted "crime against nature" punishable by a heavy fine, up to twenty years behind bars, and an eternity in hell's fire and brimstone.

"Oh my," he thought, this was exactly what his mother had in mind when she told him "that's the kind of girl who can get a boy into a lot of trouble." Aside from that, he was in Europe to make war, not love. But on the other hand, what would he tell his grandchildren when they asked, "Grampaw, what did you do in the war?" Was he going to say he was often fighting for his honor in between being propositioned by gorgeous party girls? Ah, yes, what was the Parisian place where love was for sale all over the place? Then he remembered. It was Pigalle in Montmartre, the hill overlooking all Paree. GIs had nicknamed the place Pig Alley. It was where GIs were told "to pass through right quick like." Harry had no desire to be like the guy in the dirty ditty "Z—g-Z—g Daddy from gay Paree."

With that in mind, Harry did an about-face and walked, double-time, out of the Elysian Fields—so named after the heaven where all good soldiers go after they die.

He felt virtuous and truly Christian as he admired the many fountains and monuments in and around the Place de la Concorde. The palace of the French Chamber of Deputies, with representatives from all over the three-ocean French Empire, added panache to the view across the river from the Place de la Concorde. He had read somewhere that the French Empire, second only to Britain's, enlisted thousands of soldiers for the defense of the motherland. French colonial troops were said to be experts in psychological warfare. The Senegalese, for example, liked to sneak up on a two-man German outpost and quietly slit the throat of the man on guard while his partner slept. Upon awakening, the sight of his bloodied buddy could turn the survivor into a basket case. As a mentally disturbed hospital patient, he would be more of a liability than being just another stiff and cold corpse.

But enough of war—he set his mind on peace and the postwar world celebrated in the song "When the Lights Come On Again All Over the World."

And then he dwelled on the matter.

"What have I just done? I gave up bragging rights to losing my cherry in just about the most romantic spot on God's green earth! Oh well, there's always the great white lie. I remember Roy saying it was mostly virgins who bragged about their bedroom conquests. So I'll think up a great story about how good it was, back there amongst the trees and bushes and within yards of the former palace of sexy Madame de Pompadour, as well as Napoléon's oversexed sister Caroline—destined to become Queen of Naples because she slept with all the right men."

After a short daydream about being the GI Stud of the Day, Harry headed west along the river esplanade that would take him to the Eiffel Tower—for many years the world's tallest structure. On his way to Paris' signature tourist destination, he spotted a bomb crater. Even though Paris had been declared an open city, it was nevertheless bombed—but nothing like the other capitals in war-torn Europe. There were only a few bomb craters along the Seine River, as well as a splattering of bullet holes in the Notre Dame Cathedral facade. Damage also was notable in the Place de la Concorde's cities of France monuments.

The line in front of the tower was short. Within minutes, Harry climbed into an elevator and was thrilled to a bird's-eye view of the wonderfully laid-out capital of France. There was the River Seine, its Bohemian left bank, ritzy right bank, the hill of Montmartre with its gleaming-white minaretlike spires of the Sacré Coeur.

Harry took out his map so he could better understand what he was seeing. It became clear that he was seeing the domes of Napoléon's tomb and the Sorbonne University, as well as the little island with its Notre Dame Cathedral. Then there was the Place d'Etoile—or Star Plaza—with several wide tree-lined boulevards radiating from the Arc de Triomphe.

After a half hour at the top of the arch, Harry continued on to Napoléon's tomb, deliberately designed so that it can be viewed only after bowing your head. Unlike prewar times, the tomb was minus that of Napoléon's son, the King of Rome. Hitler had returned the latter's remains to Austria.

As he studied the emperor's tomb, Harry recalled the story about Hitler's visit. Seeing Napoléon's tomb was the highlight of Hitler's tour of newly conquered Paris. A story goes that Hitler bragged about conquering most of Europe and was now contemplating an invasion of Russia. When Napoléon made no response, Hitler demanded to know why. Napoléon explained, "I am silent because I am now planning *your* tomb."

Next stop was quite some distance away—the twin spires of Notre Dame Cathedral, where one of its treasures is the crown of thorns from the Crucifixion. The crown looked more like broken-up ancient straw, but its gold wire and gem wrapping was rather splendid. Harry moved on in order to burn a candle for the folks back home, especially his ailing stepfather, Wayne.

By the time Harry had finished his exploration of Parisian landmarks, the twilight sky was turning lavender and pink. It was time to return to the hotel, where Roy was waiting and eager to tell Harry about "I found a great cafe you will like. It's down in a spooky cave strictly out of Halloween, and they call it the Cave d'Horreurs, or Cave of Horrors. That's horrors, not whores, kid. The main performer is a pianist from Boston and proud of her Ava Gardner looks and Betty Grable legs. What a dish! And she sure can tinkle them ivories."

The cafe-cum-show was in the Marais district—once chockablock with mansions owned by wealthy Jews. The years under Nazi rule had obliterated Marais's Jewish orientation. What remained were broken-down skeletons of what had been a glorious past. Anyway, the cafe was warm and cozy with a festive bluish light from all the cigarettes being smoked.

"The French would rather smoke than eat," Roy observed.

At the piano was aforementioned Bostonian singing bawdy songs about gay Paree, like the piece about a French girl "no English she could speak."

So she "carried on with a *oui, oui* for this thing, *oui, oui* for that thing, and when she gets excited, she *wee-wees* all over the place."

As soon as the customers were in a mellow mood, the Bostonian expatriate filled the room with classical masterpieces first performed in Paris by Polish expatriate Frédéric-François Chopin. Eventually, Molly switched to American pop tunes: "Symphony," "A Small Café Ma'mzelle," and "Sentimental Journey."

When it was time for a break, Roy introduced Harry as "a farm boy who is never gonna be happy down on the farm now that he's seen Paree."

"I know exactly where that's coming from," came the answer, and then, "Hello, I'm Molly Mazzelli, banned in Boston for throwing an out-of-control birthday party. After the police raid and all that stupid criminal court s—t, my aunt sent me to study music at the Sorbonne. I had to promise never to return to Boston until Paris had civilized me enough to be a concert pianist instead of being a family disgrace."

Harry liked Molly straightaway. It was as if he had always known her, he felt totally at ease in her presence.

Just after Molly's solo performance, Harry and his GI buddy were invited to a dungeon once owned by the Marquis de Sade—namesake for "sadism." The room was dark and gloomy as befits a place of horror—and so the club's name became Cave d'Horreurs. Shortly after the trio's arrival, a blood-red curtain opened on a stage occupied by a huge guillotine. A black-hooded actor dressed as a French Revolution executioner began using the guillotine blade for slicing cabbage heads. Then he invited volunteers to lose their heads. A young woman, probably a plant, got up from the audience and placed her head on the execution block. Suddenly, she waved her hands as if she had changed her mind and now feared having her head chopped off. Instead, she only wanted the executioner's head basket to be placed in the proper position to catch her lopped-off head. Then the blade dropped, and the woman's head remained intact.

"This is so boring," Molly said. "No talent. Let's get out of this toilet and go see somewhere with a little action. Pigalle, here we come."

"Pigalle," Roy said, "you mean what the guys call Pig Alley, and we are told just to pass through that place real quick like?"

"You got that right. Scared to go 'cuz you might get raped, soldier boy?"

"Hell, no," said Roy, "you *can't* rape the willing."

"I dare us," Harry countered. So off they went into streets made all the more dramatic by its darkness and sinister aura.

After a short walk, they spotted a street barrier of curved steel known as a pissoir. This was one of Baron Haussmann's urban renewal inventions, along with the iron grilles that made it possible to water and fertilize the thousands of trees all over Paris.

"Hold it," said Roy, "I gotta go."

So, holding Molly's right hand with Roy's left, he used his free hand to urinate just inside the pissoir wall. There was a rather pleasant tinkling sound against the pissoir wall as Roy emptied his bladder. Roy may have thought the pissoir an okay thing, but Madame de Gaulle considered them an affront to Parisian dignity. She had them torn down and replaced with street toilets offering more privacy.

A short promenade later and the trio arrived in front of a low-slung building with a windmill on top. The windmill was brightened with lots of red lightbulbs.

"So here we are," Molly said, "the Moulin Rouge or Red Windmill, home of high-kicking cancan girls."

Sure enough, immediately upon entry, a chorus line of full-skirted dancers kicked up their heels in a wild demonstration of the dance, which once shocked all Paris, to say nothing of the rest of the world.

"Now get a load of what's next," Molly said. "This act is the reason I brought you here. The way Roy is built, I can get him a spot in the cast if he wants to come back after his discharge."

"Wow! Great! I'm beginning to love this town," Roy said.

The red velvet curtain parted and out stepped a well-built young man wearing a tiny loincloth that covered but did not conceal his manliness. "Introducing Mr. Africa and his trained gorilla," said the master of ceremonies.

With that, the muscle man flexed a bit. Then he took the leash of his supposedly trained primate. All of a sudden, the gorilla broke loose, charged into the audience, and grabbed a little old blue-haired lady. She screamed and ran for her life, the gorilla—actually a man in a monkey suit—right after her. The animal first pulled off the old woman's wig and long golden locks fell to her shoulders, now be stripped of clothing. Her screams subsided as she slowly had all her clothes ripped off, thus revealing a naked young lady, truly a work of art worthy of an ancient Greek sculptor.

"This dump is just as boring as the last one," Molly said. "I know another place. Le Club Sexy. That ought to tell you something."

"Let's go," Harry and Roy said, almost in unison.

Harry was stopped by the Club Sexy doorman because, he said, "You're too young to come in here."

"In Paris," Harry said, "everybody looks younger than springtime."

"Okay, GI Joe. Come on in."

On stage was an Apache dancer with all the exotic, erotic moves of a modern-day Marquis de Sade. The girl being tossed around by a tough-looking dance partner couldn't keep her eyes off Roy. She suddenly dumped her partner, grabbed Roy, and did her best moves. Roy, thanks to his Afro-Haitian-Bahamian genes, was more than up to her choreographic tricks. The two of them made quite a splash, followed by the girl's invitation to have her clothes removed by Roy's eager hands. After she was down to minipanties, the girl turned and ran to her dressing room. Roy started to follow, but was stopped cold by Molly.

"Did she push all the right buttons?" Molly asked.

"Is the pope Catholic?"

"Wanta do something about it?"

"Whatcha got in mind?"

"Come to my place after doing what Parisians do to call it a night."

"Meaning what?"

"You'll see. *Suivez-moi.*"

The three of them wandered down narrow tree-lined streets to the public market Les Halles, where truckloads of produce and meat were being predawn delivered for the daily food shopping errands of the typical Parisian housewife.

"Let's stop here," Molly said as she stepped beside a small stand selling onion soup with thick layers of gooey cheese.

After soup, Molly put her arm on Roy's shoulder and gave him that certain look that meant it was time for Harry to go his own way. Harry could take a hint; a ton of bricks didn't have to fall on him. He turned around and headed back to the hotel to be alone while his buddy got lucky.

On the way home, Harry was treated to one of the most memorable sights Paris can offer—the Eiffel Tower bathed in the blue lights of an army air force coterie of searchlights. Ordinarily, the searchlights would be looking for enemy aircraft. But this was the night of September 2, 1945. On that day, the USS *Missouri* dropped anchor in Tokyo Bay and received the unconditional surrender of Japan. The paperwork was over and so was World War II officially a matter of history. It was a night to celebrate, to party, to eat, drink, and be merry; and Harry did a fine job of doing all that and more.

Next day, Kevin made an early-bird appearance at the Transatlantic Club.

"You look like death warmed over," Harry said. "She must have turned you every way but loose."

"I don't want to talk about it," Kevin said. "There's something real strange about Molly that you don't want to know. You're not ready. The only thing that saved me was I got the GIs because of the tap water or food or something. Soon as I get a chance, I'm headed for sick call for some of that pink stuff that's supposed to bind you up and stop the damn trips to the john."

"After that, are you game for the eleven o'clock Versailles tour?"

"Sounds good to me. It'll get my mind off the runs. Anyway, they should have decent toilets in the biggest and most expensive palace ever built."

Harry was awed by the immense size of Versailles and surrounding gardens, fountains, and forests. Almost all of the palace furnishings were missing, but the building was nonetheless magnificent. Even the exterior proclaimed French superiority in engineering the largest and most beautiful of European palaces. There, before Harry's wide-awake eyes, was a majestic display of Roman-style sand-colored facades topped by French-style roofs. The fine ornaments, pink marble columns, and chimney-topped roofs punctuated a display of all the best in baroque. Harry was told by his guide to imagine Versailles when the stones were golden, the bricks red, and some of the rooftops and domes leafed in pure gold. The overwhelming experience of visiting Versailles was reinforced by a wide terrace taking up the center of the facade on the palace's main floor. But it was the Hall of Mirrors that made Harry suddenly aware of what history classes back in Burnham High were all about. The hall was in a poor state of repair due to the war, but Harry nevertheless felt history lessons come to life and to have real meaning, causes, and effects. It was in this place, overlooking spacious gardens and scores of fountains, that the United States came to be. A quick look at the guidebook and Harry learned that the 1783 signing of the Treaty of Paris put an end to the American Revolution and confirmed the independence of the United States of America. It was also right here in 1871 that the King of Prussia was proclaimed Emperor—or Kaiser—of the newly created Empire of Germany. The Kaiser lost his title—and his empire was trashed—in the same hallway, for in 1919, the Treaty of Versailles ended World War I. Sadly, the same agreement paved the way to Adolf Hitler and World War II. All of a sudden, having to learn long lists of boring dates connected to boring happening made sense. Also, Harry thought it seemed especially appropriate that Versailles had been the venue for official ending of wars. Most world capitals went for monuments to warriors and wars. Not so Versailles with its Temple of Love and rooms dedicated to such mythological lovers as goddess of love Venus, her son Cupid, lover sun god Apollo, and huntress Diana. Bolstering the romance of Versailles were paintings evoking the loves of Julius Caesar, Queen Cleopatra of Egypt, Venus, Apollo, and other Greek gods and goddesses.

Harry found Queen Marie Antoinette's farm village an enchanting reminder of his own rural upbringing. It was no problem to relate to the Austrian-born teenager's fascination for the world's first profession—farming. Such were Harry's thoughts as he wandered through scores of other rooms in Europe's largest palace. There, he was to see marble paneling and ceilings decorated with gilded stuccos and world-class paintings. Basically, however, the palace was Italian in design and construction. Even Italy's most celebrated painting once found a home at Versailles—the *Mona Lisa* by Leonardo da Vinci.

As General Patton said, while ensconced in an Italian mansion, "It takes the Italians to build a palace."

Be that as it may, one look at the eye-popping, ultrastylish bedroom of Queen Marie Antoinette and Roy commented, "No wonder they had a revolution."

Versailles, first city to be built exclusively as a political capital, established the fact that the French were the best city planners. Other nations made efforts to duplicate Versailles by building new capitals such as Washington, D.C., Ottawa, Brasilia, and Canberra.

On the last day of his three-day pass, Harry chose to try his luck in gambling. They say "lucky in love or lucky in cards, you can't have both." Harry had struck out in the love department, so why not try a game of chance—like placing a bet at Longchamps racetrack in the Bois de Boulogne, once a royal hunting preserve. Emperor Napoléon III turned the Bois into a London Hyde Park-like display of trees and flowers. The centerpiece was created as a wonderful artificial lake. Shortly after the Bois was opened to the public, it became notorious for games of love as well as chance. After all, marriage-shy French bachelors have come to the conclusion: "Why buy the Bois de Boulogne when you can walk in it for nothing?"

The same expression in "Americanese" goes "Why buy a cow when you can get the milk for nothing?"

The best female retort has to be "Why buy a whole pig when you can get a little piece of sausage for nothing?"

These were the thoughts going through Harry's mind as he entered the huge park that acts as the lungs of western Paris.

The Bois de Boulogne—or Boulogne Woods—proved to be a mind-boggling display of lush forests chockablock with diverse greenery and flowers.

After several minutes of debating the best betting options, Harry bet to win rather than a less-risky place or show. Within seconds, he was to lose several thousand francs. That sounds like a lot of money, but it isn't. The exchange rate at the time was several thousand francs for a U.S. dollar. Harry chose not to bet again, especially when he felt like hell. He figured it was the change in drinking water. In any case, a rush to the nearest bathroom and Harry realized that he had contracted the same "GI runs" that had sent Roy on a grand tour of second-rate restrooms, many without toilet paper.

4

Molly's Secret

A man's most open actions have a secret side to them.
—Joseph Conrad, *Under Western Eyes* (1911)

Winter turned alpine Germany into a fantasyland of jumbled peaks overlooking forested valleys punctuated with shimmering snowdrifts. In bygone days, Germany was noted for turning picture-perfect Old World towns into magical *Christkindlmarkts*. Holiday celebrants were treated to tantalizing aromas of hot chestnuts, grilled sausages, marzipan, and gingerbread—all surrounded by holiday decorations. There was no shortage of handmade gifts ranging from wreaths, music boxes, handblown glass, and wooden toys to marionettes. Germany became a romantic land defined by gemutlichkeit—or coziness. No ethnic group celebrates the holiday season with more fervor than the Germans. These people, after all, gave the world its *tannenbaum* (Christmas tree)—a tradition presented by Teutonic Prince Albert to his English wife, Queen Victoria. Sure, Germany was great at Christmastime, but most American GIs dreamed of being home for Christmas.

Especially lonely was a lieutenant befriended by Kevin and looking for help in smuggling his German girlfriend to a Christmas reunion in Frankfurt. Here was the deal: At various checkpoints, the fraulein would cuddle with Harry in the jeep's backseat and pretend to be asleep. She would be dressed in a battle fatigue jacket, wearing a proper cap, and looking like a tired pretty young woman who should not be disturbed for such nonsense as ID papers. It was illegal to speak to a German let alone burn gallons of GI gasoline so a German could have a warm fuzzy Christmas surrounded by her Teutonic compatriots and an American boyfriend. In the meantime, the properly dressed and militarily impressive lieutenant would be in the jeep's front seat alongside his underling GI driver, namely, Kevin. The latter's reason for going to Frankfurt was to have Christmas dinner with his GI brother, who also happened to be stationed in occupied West Germany.

So off they went, Harry in the backseat and on the lookout for military police, who inherited the American notion that there had to be speed limits. The German idea goes, Since cars are designed to go up to one hundred miles an hour, why not do so?

The trip ended in the ruins of a *bahnhof* that had once been the grand central station for thriving industrial Frankfurt, now reduced to a monumental pile of wrecked buildings with only a cathedral left standing. The lieutenant and his fraulein made their merry way to a white Christmas somewhere in Frankfurt, and Harry joined his buddy for an equally festive celebration at an army base. There was the usual turkey and all the fixings, but it wasn't quite as merry as Christmases are supposed to be. There was too much talk of the next war—some said it would be against Russia, many others believed Germany would rise again for a third effort to establish *Deutschland über alles* and bring reality to the anthem "Today Germany, Tomorrow the World."

And so it became time to go back to the base in stunningly lovely southern Germany. The United States occupied the most scenic part of Germany, the British the most industrial, the Russian the capital city of Berlin and environs, and the French took over the western fringe next to Alsace-Lorraine. The latter provinces were returned to Gallic administration in 1918 after having been lost to the Franco-Prussian War of 1870.

Wintertime was busy for Harry, what with keeping his fellow troops supplied with warm clothing and keeping up with their tastes for European luxury goods on sale at the squadron PX—or post exchange.

Harry needed a break. Paris had installed a taste for travel and exploration of the continent which most influenced the planet. Harry made short rift of the paperwork required for a one-week furlough to Switzerland. He even got to list his friend Kevin on the Swiss-trip list. There was just one hassle—no transportation to the Swiss border at Basle. So it took Yankee ingenuity to travel by jeep, on the back of trucks, and even clustered on top of tanks—but the group made it to Basle. That was the good news. The bad news was being separated from Kevin, meaning Harry would have to make new friends and be without the pleasure of mutual travel experiences.

In any case, all of the furloughed GIs were treated to a fast-moving electric train about to race through a neutral land where peace, neutrality, and prosperity were the norm for many decades. As for the electric trains, the guys were warned to be careful crossing tracks "because Swiss trains are as fast as they are silent. They can be deadly if you don't watch out for yourself."

Mountain after mountain, tunnel after tunnel, jagged peaks, fir forests, eddying rivers, wide-open expanses of rugged countryside, and finally the train pulled into urbane Lucerne—also known as Luzern. This city has been called a traveler's dream come true. Its placid lake and the sunrise over Mount Pilatus have enchanted countless hikers, artists, and writers—among them, Mark Twain. Unfortunately the sky was cloudy; it was too overcast to see much of anything. There was only one visible and famous landmark to check out—the fourteenth-century Kapellbrücke. This was a wood-covered bridge decorated with Swiss historical scenes. Although sightseeing was limited, the fresh food—especially eggs, cheese, and milk—made all the difference. Harry became quickly enamored of Swiss expertise in hospitality. He learned that no one was allowed to wait table until he or she had been trained for several weeks to a year or even more. As for a German invasion, there was little fear. Every able-bodied Swiss was trained and equipped with firearms to defend his country at any moment.

Harry would never see Mount Pilatus or chill out in a cozy Lucerne nightclub. But he could send postcards with the pretty stamps of prewar days—no more single sheets of light blue V-mail. When he wrote "USA" as an address, however, the Swiss hotel clerk presented a geographical challenge.

"Which USA do you mean?"

"Which USA? I don't get it."

"There are two—the Union of South Africa and the United States of America."

"Oh, now I get it. The U.S. of America then."

Another point of contention was the constant inquiries about the well-being of Germans. The Swiss, after all, were 80 percent of German origin. So not a few were inclined to be pro-German, maybe even Nazi sympathizers. Harry had been brainwashed to hate Germans, so he was not too appreciative of Swiss backing of their German cousins.

Early the morning after arrival in Lucerne, it was time to head for Switzerland's largest city, Zurich—a world-class financial center where everybody seemed to be wealthy and carefree. As one GI put it, "Zurich is Cleveland with mountains."

Harry was assigned to the ultraluxurious Dolder Waldhaus—the most elegant surroundings of his life. There was food to match and at least one menu item suffered in translation. He found out that his *omlette d'espinards* meant "spinach omelet" in English.

After his gourmet lunch with a garden/forest view, it was time to explore the fanciest shopping street he could imagine—the Bahnhofstrasse, or Railroad Street, leading from the railroad terminal to the Zurich Sea and nearby Limmat River. What a stunning setting for shopping! First off, Harry entered Zemoli, a department store where he thought he would get good buys on Switzerland's specialty—first-class chronograph watches. Harry thought he was being clever by telling the shop clerk he wanted "watches with black faces." That was because Russian troops liked black-faced watches. They also liked to party—like the time Kevin went to drink vodka with Russians who shared in the occupation, and Kevin got too drunk. On the way back to the Hessental base, Kevin passed out and spent the night sleeping in a ditch. But that was another of his Russian stories. Right now, Harry was out to make money on the situation. He thought he was the first to be informed enough to order black-faced chronographs, but the shop clerk cut to the quick with "Yes, I know. Business watches for selling to the Russians. This one is twenty francs, here's one more expensive, and whatever I have left from the steady stream of you guys doing business with the Russians."

The "business watches" having been acquired, it was time to sightsee. He walked to the corners of Zurich where James Joyce wrote *Ulysses* and exiled Vladimir Lenin read Karl Marx and dreamed of revolution. Despite all this avant-garde radicalism, Zurich remained a bastion of deep capitalism—Bahnhofstrasse, or Railroad Street, being the heart and soul of making big money.

Since it was February, it was time to chill out with snow, sun, and skiing at its best. In addition to that, the U.S. Army encouraged three days of professional Swiss skiing lessons in such resorts as Andermatt and Engelberg—all these being next on Harry's list of destinations.

Andermatt, near the Italian border, was as mind-boggling as it gets. There was nothing in wintertime Europe as cozy as falling asleep under a feather-bed coverlet after a skiing lesson on sunny, snowy slopes chockablock with stone and timber-roofed chalets. Onion-top spires of a little church added just the right touch to a scene that deserved to be immortalized in a great painting.

Among Harry's ski school companions were three uniformed women who had been stationed in Paris. As it turned out, the women were celebrating before returning to the United States. Previously, they had staffed the Red Cross clubs, open free of charge to GIs on leave.

Harry thought it was a real treat to bond with women other than prostitutes for a change. There was only one problem. Red Cross women were famous for being off-limits to other than commissioned officers. Harry was a mere tech sergeant, a couple of shots below the top rank in noncommissioned officers—or noncoms. He had more than that going for him however. Harry was cute and funny. That'll work. So one evening before a fireplace and tables of wine and fondue cheese dip, Harry got to ask the Red Cross people if they knew his Transatlantic Club, run by the Red Cross at Place de la République. Not only did they know the club, two of them had been stationed there. Next question: Did anyone, by chance, know a Bostonian expatriate-entertainer with the name Molly Mazzelli?

There again, Harry lucked out.

One of the women let go a howl of derision and said, "You mean Molly with the Ava Gardner face and the Betty Grable gams?"

"Who else?"

"Well, I have a little surprise for you. Molly was also the buddy of a notorious French baron with a chateau in Normandy. The baron was as queer as Molly, so I suspect the two of them were more than buddies."

"No wonder Roy thought Molly was crazy."

"You don't know the half of it. Well, maybe the Molly half. The other part was Bobby, not Molly. Bobby once told me he felt like a woman trapped in a man's body."

"Oh my god. I can see where you are going with this."

Harry didn't want any further details, so he changed the subject to tomorrow's ski session in nearby Engelberg. It ended with a graduation pin showing alpine peaks and the Swiss national flag in reverse Red Cross colors—the cross being white and the background red in the case of Switzerland's national banner.

A few years later, Molly/Bobby was to show up in Hollywood, Florida—a 1950s gangster town and the haunt of such celebrated mafiosi as Frank Costello, Jimmy Blue Eyes, Al Capone, and Meyer Lansky. Mix this group with Midwesterners, including Harry, and you had the latest trend in demographics. In fact, Harry was to exaggerate that he met more fellow Buckeyes in Florida than in Ohio.

5

The Magic Album

What matters in life is not what happens to you, but what you remember and how you remember.
—Gabriel García Márquez, 1982 Nobel Prize Winner

Oh, to be in England now that spring is here. For that and other reasons, Harry engineered his greatest gift from the rich uncle he had turned into his personal travel agent. Harry, by now a staff sergeant in charge of supply and a post exchange for an entire squadron of men, sought more challenges. So what do most people want when they have got it made? Travel, that's what. Since Harry's mother hailed from England, it was no problem to arrange what the army called compassionate leave. Harry had to pay his own fare for the Red Arrow train from Paris to London. Then he would continue on to Birmingham, England's second largest city. Birmingham's train station was located alongside the Bull Ring—for many generations the city's main market center. What a special moment for Harry! For years, he had heard his mother talk about the Bull Ring, Birmingham, and the dozens of people she had left behind. So now he was to have firsthand familiarity with a host of tantalizing tales from a mother who had that magical English talent for storytelling.

First step toward fulfillment of a lifelong dream was to hail a taxi to his cousin's home in Hall Green, Birmingham. It turned out to be a pleasant neighborhood with a shopping area called the Parade. Although his cousin's semidetached home had been bombed, the dwelling had been rebuilt better than ever.

What a thrill to be about to meet his favorite pen pals, three maiden aunts who lived the life of Riley in Hall Green's pleasant parklike setting.

But it wasn't much of a thrill to his cousin Gertie Etherington, who answered the door knock.

"Oh," she said, with typical English aplomb, "you must be our cousin from America."

Funny thing about the English, they can be so composed and, at the same time, disconnected with any problem. The English, after all, don't have problems; they have "situations." They are also noted for muddling through their many wars, losing every battle except the last. Their German cousins, to the contrary, win every battle except the last. After these thoughts raced through his head, Harry sputtered, "You didn't get my card from Germany?"

"No, but it's just as well. We were expecting you at just about any time. So welcome. Come on in."

Harry apologized when he remembered his mother's caution: "You don't just drop by a friend's house the way Americans do. In England, you don't visit unless you are invited."

As soon as Harry settled in, his cousins took him out to dinner "at a place where all the English girls used to take their American soldier boyfriends. We never dreamed we would be doing that."

After dinner in a pleasant eatery near the Bull Ring marketplace, it was time to make plans to visit the family's ancestral home near Redditch, several miles from Brum. The latter is the somewhat derogatory nickname for Birmingham. The nickname was derived from the working-class word for Birmingham—"Brummagem." Thus, "koom from Broom" was the way of the working classes to reveal their origins as an official Brummy.

The next morning provided the biggest of all Harry's travel thrills and chills—arrival by bus at Gorcott Hill, the closest point to ancestral home the twelfth-century Gorcott Hall midway on the side of Gorcott Hill. Gone was the moat once used for protection from Middle Ages invasions and battles. But all the other antiquities were in their full glory. First to attract Harry's attention was a drawing room window with 365 panes of leaded glass—one glass for each day of the year. "My mother counted them," said Harry, "and she claimed there are more than 365 panes."

"Did she tell you about this?" Gertie asked, pointing to a circular piece of stained glass protected by what looked like chicken wire.

"That must be from Good Queen Bess," Harry said with more than a hint of pride in remembering Florrie's description of her childhood home.

"That's right. She stayed here as a stop before going on to nearby Kenilworth Castle to see her boyfriend, the Earl. When she left, she gave Gorcott a gift—her coat of arms painted on glass. Now come see her favorite room."

The latter proved to be a small side room with a fireplace setting used for an English high tea in honor of Harry's visit. After tea, there was a grand tour, things like the fourteenth-century section with bricked up windows.

That was because the king levied a window tax on the theory that if people were rich enough to have glass windows, they could afford to contribute to the royal tax till.

The following day was banquet time. Harry was impressed by the long hours of food preparation in the buttery just to the east of the main salon. Another of his cousins, Olive Yeomans, had gone hunting for venison destined to be a main course in a dining fete fit for royalty. When Harry saw the great hall table chockablock with colorful displays of rare and wonderful eats, he began to wonder if the British had suffered all that much from the war. A British soldier, also one of the honored guests, let the cat out of the bag when he exclaimed, "Real butter! I haven't seen that since I was a kid."

As for the sugary treats, they were made available—in part—by the ration tickets Harry had been given prior to Uncle Sam's compassionate leave package tour, so to speak. To put it mildly, it was a dinner to be remembered forever.

And then it happened. As Harry was introduced to "rellys," one after the other, he began to wonder, "Who are all these strangers? Can they really be related to me somehow?"

Only family albums brought the scene into focus. There was Harry, along with Florrie, his mother, and Gladys, his aunt, both back in the United States of America. To see his baby pictures along with those of his newly discovered English relatives made everything come to light. Harry's mind went back to the sunny day in Schwäbisch Gmund, Germany, when he put together an album of pictures from his European trips for free, courtesy of Uncle Sam. They included photos of his best friend as well as other buddies in uniform. Harry vowed then and there to give special treatment to family pictures. Over the years, he heard over and over again that family photographs are the best things to save from fires, earthquakes, and/or other disasters. Material things can be replaced. But family pictures are irreplaceable treasures for years and years.

In any case, finding a ready-made family in England made Harry feel all the more at home. It was almost as if there were no five thousand miles between his English relatives and those back in Ohio. Harry's newfound sense of freedom was quite another culture shock. While standing in front of Windsor Castle's royal chapel, he was confronted with a Do Not Enter sign. Along came an Englishwoman who smiled and said, "Go ahead. Ignore the bloody sign. You Yanks can do anything you like while you're over here." So true! As an American abroad, Harry was not held back by European rules and regulations. By the same token, he was not in America and therefore not obliged to put up with that country's sometimes peculiar, if not outdated, laws. It was the American expatriate's sense of freedom that fueled many works of art, especially in France.

After meeting the English "rellys," it was travel time in the hills and meadows of castle-rich England. The visit to William Shakespeare's birthplace was a must. Since Shakespeare lived so close to Harry's midland relatives, he wondered if he might be related to the world's most celebrated writer. Wouldn't that be great?—especially since Harry intended to become a writer. Just being English seemed a head start into the world of literature and drama. After all, Britain's weather is so bad that the English have nothing better to do than stay inside and write—or go on stage and act. That's why, Harry assumed, Great Britain produces some of the world's best writers and actors.

All too soon, it was time to leave relatives behind and board the train for London—first leg of a return to Germany. It was in Victoria Station that he heard a cruel put-down of England's beloved wartime monarch. Although the comment was meant to be harmless, it went deeper than that when someone tapped Harry on the shoulder and said, "If you hurry, you might get a chance to see stuttering George." The cruel comment referred to the king's speech impediment. King George VI was never intended or expected to be king-emperor, so there was no need for him to be a world-class public speaker. However, when his older brother, Edward VIII, married a twice-wed American commoner, it was time to dethrone Edward and give the crown to the unprepared number 2 son, known to close friends and family as Bertie. He chose to be royally known as King George VI. His queen consort, later Queen Elizabeth the Queen Mother, taught her husband to control his stuttering. He eventually became a more than adequate public speaker. From that point on, the king became one of the most beloved and respected monarchs in British history. For training the king and other accomplishments, Hitler called Britain's World War II queen "the most dangerous woman in Europe." In any case, as a first-generation Anglo-American, Harry was destined to eventually meet and photograph British royals, and these opportunities were to be among the most memorable occasions of his life!

By late summer, it was time to leave Europe and go back to America. Instead of a converted luxury liner, Harry sailed homeward in a beat-up Victory ship—vessels built poorly and in haste in order to fill a need for merchant ships as soon as possible. In any case, the Victory ship set sail from Bremerhaven, Germany, on July 25, 1946, and arrived in New York on August 2, 1946.

Steaming into New York harbor with its special gift from France—the Statue of Liberty—became one of Harry's most dramatic occasions.

After riding the rails from New York to Fort Meade, Maryland, there was a fast-forward conclusion of Harry's military career. By August 7, 1946, he was honorably discharged. That meant travel expenses home to Toledo and separation funds totaling $512.95. At the time, that was BIG MONEY. Harry felt rich. Aside from hundreds of dollars in cash, he had a barracks bag filled with Euro loot—a German portable Erika-Naumann typewriter, perfumes from Paris, a Zeiss camera from Germany, and scads of pictures. Wow! Only a year before, he earned 7.50 cents an hour by working at Grey's Greenhouse and Apiary back in Sylvania, Ohio. It seemed magical to suddenly have hundreds of dollars in savings. But then, of course, he was still a kid. When you are a youngster, just about everything seems magical.

Harry marveled at the way his army time seemed short yet so filled with lots of unexpected travel, *camaraderie*, and high rank. His rapid rise in rank was a metaphor of Nazi Germany's blitzkrieg—or lightning war. During May of 1945, he was hoeing corn and slopping hogs back on the farm. By May 8, 1946, he had become a supply NCO with the rank of tech sergeant.

By August 1946, he had returned to his own Ohio farm home—and the best was yet to come, at least from the financial standpoint. That is to say, the eagle screamed loud and clear. That's army lingo for payday. If there were no women around, the eagle was said to have s—t.

To shorten a long story, my alter ego, Harry, continued to score free travel after his discharge and following college enrollment under the GI Bill. Shortly after his honorable discharge, with such decorations as a bronze Central Europe Campaign Star, Harry sought university admission. He wanted to attend the best journalistic establishment in the country, and he determined that to be Northwestern University near Hemingway's childhood home in Illinois. That school was so popular that Harry was told they might find a place for him within two or three years.

University of Toledo was Harry's next great hope. He wanted so much to be close to home and study in the shadows of TU's signature gothic towers rising from a spacious landscape of trees, lawns, and shrubbery. But a TU education was out of the question. TU had a shortage of openings, so admission was limited to Toledo taxpayers only. Harry's home was eighteen miles outside the Toledo city limits.

So Harry took on his second choice—Bowling Green State University, south of Toledo. That university could admit him if he could find a place to live in a town saturated with ex-GIs seeking free college educations. After a few hours of searching, Harry found a room over a service station and about nine blocks from the BGSU campus. The GI Bill paid all tuition and book expenses, plus a monthly fifty-dollar check equivalent to four hundred dollars in 2006 money. The money would not have been enough if Harry hadn't pledged Kappa Sigma fraternity. That meant seven-dollar-a-week dormitory digs in a two-story brick fraternity house that was the last word in campus elegance and convenience. There was always enough to chip in for a keg of beer. This bit of liquid contraband was stashed in a second-floor library. This room was off-limits by virtue of a gentleman's agreement with housemother "Mom Arthur." She "civilized" the brothers by enforced wait staff duty done in world-class style by young men properly dressed for dinner. The guys, mostly ex-servicemen, learned to serve food from the left, take away empty plates from the right, and present the main entree squarely in front of the diner.

The bottom line was formal education for free. Harry's journalism classes were just what he needed and wanted. But his passion for learning conversational French was suppressed. After a year of college French, Harry could conjugate scores of irregular verbs, but he wasn't remotely conversational. As karma would have it, Canada was having a U.S. dollar shortage. To encourage GIs to study in Canada, the nationalized rail line paid two-thirds of the train fare upon a student's return to the Unite States. So Uncle Sam provided a bargain train fare from Toledo to Québec City in French Canada. Harry was bedazzled like no tomorrow. Here he was, one more time, in a civilized Euro setting with world-class food, drink, architecture, and scenery—and almost all expenses were on his rich Uncle Sam's tab.

It doesn't end there. Uncle Sam's is a gift that keeps on giving—even as late as the 1990s during a visit to France in order to see the Normandy battlefields. Harry was admitted gratis to the Peace Memorial at Caen, capital of Normandy. Why? That's because he could show Peace Memorial documentation of his having served in France at some point during the Liberation from D-day 1944 to VE Day 1945. The name of this author, Harry Bandera's alter ego Harold Flagg, is listed for a memorial under direction of Pierre Salinger. The list of names existed in Caen at the time of Flagg's visit, but plans for a memorial have since been dropped. In any case, being a veteran of World War II rated free entrance to the Peace Memorial. Highlight of that visit was seeing the photographs of teenagers, like Harry, being hanged by SS Storm Troopers. There was also a skeletal face lighted so that it seemed to fade in and out of view. It was an image that has haunted me for many years.

And, oh yes, the free travel continued on into the year 2006. My "rich uncle" partially reimbursed me for traveling by Tri-Rail from my Fort Lauderdale home to the Veterans Administration Center in downtown Miami. The same Tri-Rail ticket was good for access to lively Miami by a fast, efficient rail system almost on par with Paris' metro. It was a joy to see Miami looking like Hong Kong on speed—new construction all over the place for miles and miles on end. My favorite hangout was Miami Bayside. I like to start with a massage and then visit the hundreds of minishops and a food court that seem like a mini-World's Fair. The whole bit teaches that humans are all alike, just a mess of bones, blood, and flesh. The only thing different is our dinners. And Bayside is chockablock with affordable—even cheap—grub ranging with Bahamian/Caribbean dishes to French crepes, Spanish paella, and Argentine steak. And then there is the picture-postcard view—blue skies and a wine-dark sea, tropical flora and fauna, and music with the hypnotic tempo of Cuban *Son*, Bahamian goombay, Calypso, mambo, rumba, or whatever new lively dance that the West Indians are about to hit the charts big-time.

EPILOGUE

They are all dead now. Well, almost all. My English-born mother, grandmother, and aunt passed away many years ago. The late Molly—real name Bobby—went through two large inheritances while having a blast in his beloved adopted hometown, Hollywood-by-the-sea-in-Florida. He died penniless and was buried gratis with full military honors in a veterans' cemetery. Roy—real name Ray—is a composite with part of his character drawn from an Afro-Bahamian entertainer. Both Ray and Roy are no longer with us.

I really miss Florrie. She was the funniest, wisest, kindest mom a GI could ever hope to have. While I was overseas, she somehow found the time to write me a letter several times a week.

As for places in this book, I wrote the Parisian scenes as if everything happened during a single visit. Truth be known, the Paris material covers three visits boiled down into what sounds like one.

Kath is the GI Joe I miss the most. He appears in this book as Kevin Lavern. His real name was Lavern Kath, and he was a Wisconsinite of German descent, just as depicted in this book. My last meeting with Kath was, like the first, in a train station. Kath—most GI relationships were on a last-name basis—had spent years trying to locate me after we had been discharged from army service. Then, one sunny morning in Fort Lauderdale, came the telephone query, "Do you know who this is?" Straightaway, I knew the voice belonged to my long-lost buddy. We chatted awhile about good and bad days of yore when we were at war. As fate would have it, I learned that Kath was slated for an Orlando convention. So I booked an Amtrak coach out of Fort Lauderdale and headed for Orlando. Is it any wonder that I love trains? They have been a "yellow brick path" to amazing adventures all through my life.

On arrival in Orlando, my train stopped far short of the terminal. Kath must have spotted me the instant I left the train. Like a lunatic under a luminous full moon, he raced across shiny steel tracks and stopped only to give me the biggest bear hug of my life. He looked me over, head to toe, and insisted, "You haven't changed a bit." I offered the same little white lie in return. After the long-postponed reunion, we joined Kath's wonderful wife, Ruth, for lunch. It was then that she told me her husband had spent many hours on one final wish before dying—to find and talk to me one last time. Sadly, my buddy was near death from prostate cancer and heart failure.

As I write this script, Miami Veterans Administration medicos are treating me for prostate cancer. At one point, I asked Dr. Pedro Bustello how much my cancer battle was costing us taxpayers. "I heard it was $40,000," I said. My doctor chuckled and said, "That's what we paid the guy who played the flute while we radiated you. The total cost was more like $90,000." At least it worked. I subsequently made a complete recovery. I now attend Fort Lauderdale Gilda's Club programs as a cancer survivor.

Sadly, Lavern Kath didn't win his cancer struggle. He passed away at age seventy-two. I have no closure; I can't quite realize that it is impossible to phone up and talk about our army adventures and misadventures.

Whenever I am alone at night, I am aware of Kath's and other souls who have passed to the other side. I am convinced that we will meet again somewhere, somehow, someway, someday. After all, Albert Einstein says we are energy, and energy cannot be created or destroyed. So when my time comes, I expect not a dark void but light and joy aided and abetted by hundreds of once-earthbound spirits. Among them will be my best writer colleague, the late war hero Hank Jones. He said, just before death, "Here it comes."

I want to think that Hank is in the most literary corner of the spirit world, waiting for me to say the same final line, "Here it comes."

As for my cancer, it may mean 30, or the related symbol #—the traditional way for an old-time newspaperman to sign off a story.

And yes, when I report for duty on the other side, I would like to be met by an angel in a tech sergeant's uniform, on tap to greet me with a big hug just outside the pearly gates train station. But that's silly—trains, when everybody has wings! Still, wouldn't it be great if there *were* railroads in heaven, train buff that I am?

It is interesting to note that trains *did* exist in the French version of Soldiers' Heaven during my last visit to Paris. That is to say, I was startled to see an old-time 40 et 8 railroad car as part of a train exhibit on the Champs-Elysées—French for "Elysian Fields," Gallic equivalent of Germany's Valhalla.

Before I pass away, I have a dream. I would like to repay at least part of what I owe my country for all that free travel and health care. If I accomplish a payback, then when I die, I deserve to live forever in tree-lined Elysian Fields.

Here's the deal:

I am a charter member and supporter of the New Orleans National World War II museum. I think it would be a joy, as well as mighty lucrative, to establish a warrior/writer Ernest Hemingway exhibit at the museum. I would love nothing more than to start the ball rolling by selling my Picasso, which appears among photos in the back of this book. My signed-in-the-stone *Tête de Femme (Jacqueline)* is shown above a newspaper article about a similar *Jacqueline* portrait. The latter came with a $4.5 million asking price at the 2006 Art Basel Miami Beach show. My asking price is much less. Make out the check to the National World War II Museum, please.

Wouldn't it be cool if someone bought my Picasso for enough money to establish a Hemingway "cash cow" to New Orleans? The idea first occurred to me during a National Endowment of the Arts tour of Hemingway's Key West in April of 2007. So unless someone has already done so, I would like to lead the way to a Hemingway exhibit in New Orleans.

And so I conclude this book with the parting words of Key West Hemingway House Museum guides: HAVE A HEMINGWAY DAY.

ENLISTED RECORD AND REPORT OF SEPARATION 7603-17
VOL 95 PAGE 16   HONORABLE DISCHARGE

1. LAST NAME—FIRST NAME—MIDDLE INITIAL	2. ARMY SERIAL NO.	3. GRADE	4. ARM OR SERVICE	5. COMPONENT
FLAGG HAROLD E	35 852 447	SGT 6 MAY 46	ARMD-F	AUS
6. ORGANIZATION	7. DATE OF SEPARATION	8. PLACE OF SEPARATION	SEPARATION CENTER	
TRP B 71ST CONST SQ	7 AUG 46	FT GEO G MEADE MD		
9. PERMANENT ADDRESS FOR MAILING PURPOSES	10. DATE OF BIRTH	11. PLACE OF BIRTH		
C/O PM BERKEY (LUCAS) OHIO	12 MAY 26	MILWAUKEE WIS		
SEE 9	12. COLOR EYES	13. COLOR HAIR	14. HEIGHT	15. WEIGHT
	BROWN	BROWN	5'9"	135 LBS

STUDENT HIGH SCHOOL ACADEMIC X-02

MILITARY HISTORY

22. DATE OF INDUCTION	23. DATE OF ENLISTMENT	24. DATE OF ENTRY INTO ACTIVE SERVICE	25. PLACE OF ENTRY INTO SERVICE
26 OCT 44		26 OCT 44	CLEVELAND OHIO

X 22 LUCAS OHIO   SEE 9

30. MILITARY OCCUPATIONAL SPECIALTY AND NO.	31. MILITARY QUALIFICATION AND DATE
SUPPLY NCO 821	SS 17 RIFLE MKM M1 RIFLE

32. BATTLES AND CAMPAIGNS
GO33WD45 CENTRAL EUROPE

33. DECORATIONS AND CITATIONS
GOOD CONDUCT MEDAL EUROPEAN AFRICAN MIDDLE EASTERN THEATER RIBBON
ARMY OCCUPATION MEDAL (GERMANY) WORLD WAR II VICTORY RIBBON

34. WOUNDS RECEIVED IN ACTION
NONE

35. LATEST IMMUNIZATION DATES			36.	SERVICE OUTSIDE CONTINENTAL U. S. AND RETURN		
SMALLPOX	TYPHOID	TETANUS	OTHER (SPECIFY)	DATE OF DEPARTURE	DESTINATION	DATE OF ARRIVAL
NOV 44	DEC 45	DEC 44	TYP DEC 45	21 APR 45	FRANCE	1 MAY 45
				25 JUL 46	UNITED STATES	2 AUG 46

37. TOTAL LENGTH OF SERVICE				38. HIGHEST GRADE HELD
CONTINENTAL SERVICE		FOREIGN SERVICE		
YEARS	MONTHS	DAYS	YEARS	MONTHS	DAYS	1-SGT

39. PRIOR SERVICE
NONE

40. REASON AND AUTHORITY FOR SEPARATION
AR 615-365 DTD 15 DEC 44 RR 1-1 & PAR 1B CIR 163 HQS 2ND ARMY 2 JUL 46

41. SERVICE SCHOOLS ATTENDED
NONE

PAY DATA   VOUCHER 4062

42. LONGEVITY FOR PAY PURPOSES	43. MUSTERING OUT PAY	44. SOLDIER DEPOSIT	45. TRAVEL PAY	46. TOTAL AMOUNT, NAME OF DISBURSING OFFICER	PEARSON
YEARS MONTHS	$300.00	$100.00	NONE	$30.45	$512.95	MAJOR FD

INSURANCE NOTICE

47. KIND OF INSURANCE			48. HOW PAID	49. EFFECTIVE DATE OF ALLOTMENT	50. DATE OF NEXT PREMIUM DUE	51. PREMIUM DUE EACH MONTH	52. INTENTION OF VETERAN TO
X			X	31 AUG 46	30 SEP 46	$6.40	X

Certificate

STATE OF OHIO, COUNTY OF LUCAS, ss:

I, Gerald J. Cullen, Recorder of Lucas County, State of Ohio, do hereby certify the foregoing to be a true and correct copy of Discharge from Military Service, as same appears on record in the office of the Lucas County Recorder.

WITNESS my hand and official-seal at Toledo, Ohio _____ SEP 16 1948

_____ Recorder.

By _____ Deputy Recorder

My honorable discharge verifies most of the information in this book.

France recognized my participation in the D-Day 1944 to VE-Day 1945 Liberation.

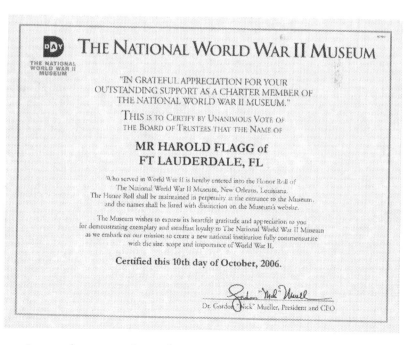

I am a charter member and supporter of the National World War II Museum.

This is my mother's favorite picture of Gorcott Hall, our ancestral home in England. It dates to the 12th century and once hosted Queen Elizabeth I.

That's me, about 5 years old and flanked by my mother, left, and Aunt Gladys. Grandma Wheatley is pretending to drive our rich uncle's new car. It's parked just in front of hops to flavor home-brewed beer.

All aboard a French 40 et 8, designed to transport 40 men and 8 horses to the battlefields of two world wars.

Me as a Tank Destroyer battalion corporal chilling out during a quiet Sunday of closed shops in Occupied West Germany.

My main base in 1945-46 was the picture postcard perfect Swäbisch Hall.

Red Cross women and I show off our newly learned skiing abilities in snowy Switzerland.

I am reaching for the French plaque honoring Ohio troops who helped liberate France from Nazi occupation.

On June 20, 1946, I went to my English ancestral home and met dozens of cousins, among them: 5-year-old Margaret, cousin Vivien's oldest daughter, plus the family sheepdog, Sally, aged 12. That's the Gorcott Hall barn in the background. I helped deliver a calf there and it was named after me.

After college and beginning in the 1950s, I became obsessed with All Things Hemingway. Here I am seated in a cigar-maker's chair in Ernest Hemingway's Key West studio.

Photo by Craig Aranha

I spent the night searching for Hemingway's spirit in his Compleat Angler room and then went hunting and fishing on the Bimini flats with Bone Fish Ray.

During many years as a Bahamas Handbook writer-editor, I shot many pictures of royals. Here is a favorite—Queen Elizabeth II in a characteristic 'watch your step' pose as she is about to dedicate a Bahamian school for tourism on the Nassau campus of the University of the West Indies. On her right is Bahamas Prime Minister the Rt. Hon. Hubert A. Ingraham, He was Prime Minister from 1992 to 2002 and re-elected in 2007. In 2008, The Queen is slated to celebrate her 35th year as Queen of The Bahamas, a responsibility she undertook on Bahamas Independence Day July 10, 1973. Few Americans and many Bahamians are aware that the Commonwealth of The Bahamas is a monarchy with a Rule of Law government matching that of the Canadian, Australian and New Zealand monarchies.

I snapped this shot of Prince Edward, looking tropical cool, as he landed on Blue Lagoon Island, a favorite tropical paradise of my brother Bob, sister-in-law Anesta, and me.

During the 1995 Royal Visit, I rated a Royal Bahamas Police Force escort to a garden party at Nassau's Government House equivalent to Buckingham Palace. I am wearing miniatures of my World War II medals as part of the dress code for the garden party.

Any takers? I would like to sell my signed-in-the-stone Picasso for seed money to establish a Hemingway exhibit in the National World War II Museum.

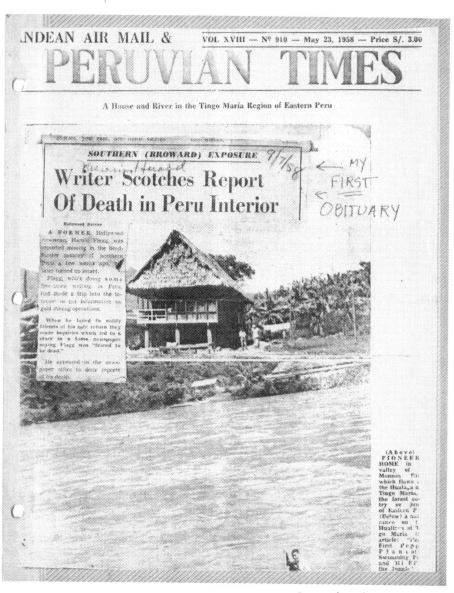

NDEAN AIR MAIL &   VOL XVIII — N° 910 — May 23, 1958 — Price S/. 3.00

PERUVIAN TIMES

A House and River in the Tingo Maria Region of Eastern Peru

SOUTHERN (BROWARD) EXPOSURE   9/7/58

Evening Herald

Writer Scotches Report Of Death in Peru Interior

← MY FIRST OBITUARY

Hollywood Bureau

A FORMER Hollywood newsman, Harold Flagg, was reported missing in the head-hunter country of northern Peru a few weeks ago, later turned up intact.

Flagg, who's doing some free-lance writing in Peru, had made a trip into the interior to get information on gold mining operations.

When he failed to notify friends of his safe return they made inquiries which led to a story in a Lima newspaper saying Flagg was "feared to be dead."

He appeared in the newspaper office to deny reports of his death.

(Above) PIONEER HOME in valley of Monzon Ri which flows the Huallaga n Tingo Maria, the forest co try or jun of Eastern P (Below) a nat canoe on Huallaga at T go Maria. article: "Pe First Pepp Plant at Swimming P and Hi F the Jungle"

Cover Photo by Harold Flagg

Reports of my death in a Peruvian jungle were an exaggeration. Instead, I was dead drunk on Pisco Sours, Peru's answer to the hydrogen bomb. It made it easier to handle the poisonous snakes, landslides, super-sized rats, blood-sucking bats and flesh-eating fish, not to mention the dreadful head-hunter neighbors.